Campus Visits
and College Interviews

Campus Visits and College Interviews

A Complete Guide for College-Bound Students and Their Families

Zola Dincin Schneider

College Entrance Examination Board
New York

In all of its book publishing activities the College Board endeavors to present the works of authors who are well qualified to write with authority on the subject at hand and to present accurate and timely information. However, the opinions, interpretations, and conclusions of the authors are their own and do not necessarily represent those of the College Board; nothing contained herein should be assumed to represent an official position of the College Board or any of its members.

Copies of this book are available from your local bookseller or may be ordered from College Board Publications, Box 886, New York, New York 10101. The price is $9.95.

Editorial inquiries concerning this book should be directed to Editorial Office, The College Board, 45 Columbus Avenue, New York, New York 10023–6917.

Grateful acknowledgment is made to the University of Montana for permission to reproduce a section of its campus map.

Library of Congress Catalog Number: 86–072713

ISBN: 0–87447–260–1

Printed in the United States of America

9 8 7 6 5 4 3 2 1

In loving memory of my parents
Renee and Herman Dincin

Contents

PART 1

The Campus Visit

PART 2

The Interview

Acknowledgments

I want to express at the outset my gratitude to Carolyn Trager, senior editor at the College Board, who conceived the idea for this book, with the hope that the result meets her expectations. Throughout, her gracious encouragement reinforced my enthusiasm for the project.

I wrote this book because campus visits and interviews have been central to my work as a consumer-oriented college adviser to high school students. *Campus Visits* is a natural outgrowth of that work and therefore owes much to the many students who used the suggestions and reported back on their efficacy. I want to thank all my students. I am especially grateful to Matt Zapruder, Ruth Polk, Eric Namrow, Nancy Clemmer, Mark Green, Cate Martin, Christine Rosenhauer, Ross Forman, and Greer Mendel for their helpful insights. Several veterans of the admissions process, now in graduate school and beyond, Eric Duskin, Jonathon Levy, Seth Grimes, and Louis DeSipio, and others who are college bound, Ben Lewit and Joe Edelheit, contributed their constructive ideas.

My special appreciation is also due to many others who helped along the way. To the college admissions counselors who gave so freely of their thoughts and expertise, especially Richard Stewart, Wallace Ayers, Carol Wheatley, Simone Stevens, Bonita Washington, Deborah Wright, Sarah Greenfield, and Valerie Raines Bell, I am most grateful. I also want to thank that band of friends and specialists who contributed to various aspects of the book—Rhona Hartman, Maxine Krulwich, Barbara Mendel, Claire Sprague, Jane Lewit, Barbara Zelenko, Robert Gillman, Rhoda Wolf, Afaf Mahfouz, Gerrie and Len Pearlin, Rita Reaves, Mike Curzan, and Gloria Stern—who were all so generous with their encouragement and suggestions.

I am especially thankful to Daniel Schneider for his ready assistance and expert research, to Linda Kanefield for her caring interest and careful reading, and to Peter Schneider for his enthusiastic support and wise counsel. There is no end to my indebtedness to Norman Schneider for his patience in teaching me the wonders of Agnes, my word processor, for his timely intervention in rescuing me from my computer mishaps, for his ingenuity in formatting the book, and for his many helpful suggestions.

I am most grateful to Gail Forman, my friend and first line-reader, who with sharpened pencil and practiced eye went over the manuscript, finding all my syntactical errors and nonparallel constructions. I especially value the devoted support and family advice of Dian Dincin Buckman, who was so instrumental in the formation of this book project.

Above all, few words can express my pleasure at having Irving Schneider at my side as my severest critic, best adviser, and valued companion. Throughout this writing he maintained his good humor and patience and was always willing to read, yet one more time, the pages as they grew into a book.

Of course, in the end, I alone am responsible for the contents. It goes without saying that I have attempted to ensure the anonymity of all persons mentioned in this book.

Zola Dincin Schneider

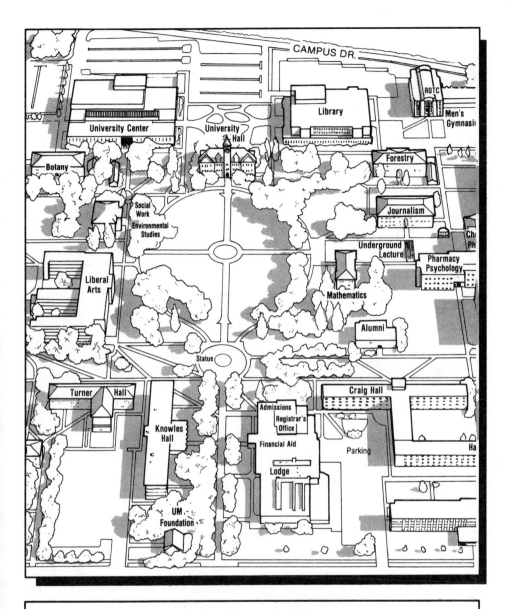

PART 1

The Campus Visit

Chapter 1

Deciding to Go

Why You Should Go

Connie, Doug, Jeff, and Mandy, students at different high schools, all shared the same concern: Not one of them had any notion of what a college was actually like. They had read the vital statistics about various colleges listed in the big, comprehensive directories, gone through the descriptive guides from cover to cover to get a sense of the ambience at those colleges, talked to a few friends about their colleges when they were home on vacation, but they still didn't know what a college was really like or how it felt to be on a campus and away from home.

Connie's first notions of college came from listening to her sister and her friends talk about their experiences, and each one wanted Connie to apply to the college she was attending. Although each made a good case for the college she had chosen, Connie knew that she needed to check them out for herself since she didn't think that what suited them would necessarily suit her.

Doug, a student at a large metropolitan high school, decided that a college in a small town offered few distractions and would therefore be more conducive to studying. Yet, when he made his visits to the colleges he had chosen, he was struck

3

by how frustrated he felt at not having a wide choice of movies or foreign restaurants nearby. He realized that although the students he met liked the closeness and togetherness of the college environment, he needed the variety of choices available in a larger community. To test out his revised priorities, he embarked on visits to his state university and to smaller urban colleges to see what they would be like.

Jeff, on the other hand, had little idea of what type of college suited him. He thought that a small college would offer him good contact with faculty and he would get to know most, if not all, of the students quite well; but he also imagined that a large university would have a broad range of academic courses and social activities from which to choose. He decided that a serious investigation of different types of colleges was called for so that he could determine what best matched his interests.

Mandy's mother had always spoken enthusiastically about the wonderful education she had received at a women's college, but Mandy resisted the idea of going to a single-sex school. To placate her mother, however, she arranged for a campus visit and interview at her mother's alma mater. Much to her surprise, she found herself talking easily to the admissions counselor about her reluctance to go to a women's college and her long-time ambition to become a lawyer. Afterward, Mandy stayed overnight with two sophomores, one from a small town in Georgia and the other from Chicago, talking most of the night about the advantages and the drawbacks of the college. They were frank and funny about a lot of the campus doings. Although Mandy and the two students came from dissimilar backgrounds, she was delighted to find that they shared an interest in mystery novels and funky earrings. The next morning she sat in on two classes and was enthusiastic about the give and take of the discussion. Pleased by what she was discovering, Mandy decided to put her mother's college on her own list of schools to consider seriously.

These four students were getting a good start on their college search. Sometimes high school students are so uptight about college that they forget that they control their own choices. Students can, and must, determine for themselves which colleges are best for them and not choose a college because it is well known or popular. It is essential for students to figure out which colleges match *their* needs, desires, and aspirations.

Once upon a time, young people went to colleges that their parents picked out for them, or ones closest to home, or ones that cousins or friends said were "just great." But times have changed. Students now realize that choosing a college is a big decision that will affect their lifelong interests, careers, and friendships. They are looking for colleges where they can be successful academically, stimulated intellectually, and happy socially; where they can learn, grow, and make friends.

To find the right colleges, students must be good shoppers, especially now when a year at college can cost as much as a car. Just as no one chooses a car without a test drive, no one should choose a college without a test visit. Reading, talking, or thinking about colleges doesn't replace the road test: the campus visit. Visits give students personal insight into the campus style, student body, social atmosphere, available facilities, and academic dynamics. Visits to a number of colleges make it possible to compare them and to evaluate to what extent they match students' requirements. Visits answer the question a college shopper should be asking: "What would it be like for me to go to college here?"

Who Should Go When

Jim and Annalee, two junior-year honors students with heavy academic programs, were worried about the timing of their campus visits. Their top-rated colleges weren't holding interviews between January and June, not much would be happening on campuses during the summer, and they weren't sure they could take time out from school the following fall. They talked to their high school counselor who showed them the next year's academic calendar, and they saw that there were four autumn school holidays, including Labor Day, when they could conveniently make campus visits. They compared the colleges' academic calendars and found that the colleges would be in session on those holidays. Aware that campuses are lively places to visit in early fall, and that interview appointments are best booked early at the more selective colleges, Jim and Annalee got busy.

Mike, a varsity high school soccer player, hoped he'd make a college team. Since he practiced every day from mid-August through the fall, he had to plan his college trips during his junior year spring vacation or after the soccer season was over. Luckily, when he called for appointments with the coaches, he found that the colleges were in session during his spring holiday and he would have a chance to talk to players and have his interviews at the same time.

On the other hand, Liz, a brass player in the school band, waited until her senior year before researching colleges. When she was a junior, she had gone with the band to Boston, and had briefly ambled around Back Bay and wandered onto a campus. She had liked what she saw, but knew she would have to devote much more time and energy to serious college visits. She reviewed the band schedule and determined some dates for visits when she wouldn't be involved with rehearsals.

All these students were doing sound planning. Each was devising a schedule appropriate to his or her needs, for there is more than one right time to make campus visits. The one essential factor is that the college be *in session.*

During School Week

Juniors and seniors must be purposeful college shoppers. They should explore colleges when things are buzzing: when classes are meeting, students are studying, and ordinary day-to-day activities are taking place. This means making visits during the school week.

High School Holidays

Since junior and senior years are also intense academic periods, it is important to balance high school requirements with college trips and schedule visits so that not too many school days are missed. *High school holidays are choice opportunities for college visits.* National holidays, especially those falling on Mondays when colleges are generally in session, are appropriate times. A good plan is to travel on Sunday and be on campus Monday. If several colleges are on the itinerary, Tuesday and Wednesday could be added. The early part of the week—Monday through Thursday—is ideal for campus visits because things are bustling then.

Spring Vacation

Juniors who have researched the colleges (see Chapter 6, *How to Read a College Catalog*) and put in the time to analyze their needs and requirements (see Chapter 10, *Putting Your Best Foot Forward*) may consider using their spring vacation for college visits. Players of fall sports, and students considering early action or early decision with application deadlines in November of their senior year, should use these opportune holidays, but should check well in advance to make certain the colleges are in session and that their admissions staffs say it's okay to visit.

Best Seasons

Late summer and early September before senior year begins are convenient times to visit since many colleges begin their fall semester as early as mid-August. But generally, fall through winter and sometimes early spring are the seasons when seniors should conduct their major explorations.

Before Applications

Your campus expeditions should determine whether or not you will apply to the colleges, so *make your visits before applications are due.* As most application deadlines range from January 1 through March of senior year, plan accordingly. Colleges that have late spring deadlines may be visited later.

After Acceptances

You may decide to postpone visits until after you've received acceptances. Keep in mind that if you wait until then you may have only the two weeks from April 15 (when many decision notices arrive) to May 1 (the reply date specified by most colleges) to make your decision about which college to attend. Delaying your first campus look may put you in a tight bind.

Many colleges invite their accepted candidates to spend a few days on campus before the May 1 reply date to encourage them to enroll. This can be a good time to review your opinion about the colleges that have accepted you and to make some in-depth comparisons.

When Not to Go

Steve and two high school buddies took the family car on a warm summer afternoon and drove to the University of Santa Cruz, intending to get an impression of the residential college system it offered. They thought they would look around and talk to students and faculty about the way the college worked, take a look at the dorms, gym, cafeteria, and science labs, and pick up catalogs.

But look was all they could do. The college, except for the admissions office, was shut up tight and all they saw was the outside of buildings and the beautiful campus with its view of Monterey Bay. They had not accomplished their main purpose.

As important as when to visit colleges is when not to visit. It is bad timing to go during reading period or exams, when classes and activities cease and students are too frazzled to pay attention to visitors.

Weekends, though a convenient time for high school students to visit, are days to avoid if you want to see more than the party life of a college. By 4 p.m. on Friday afternoon admissions staff, faculty, and students are keyed up for social activities, and they may seem to be rushing their meetings with you. Interviews are better scheduled for more leisurely days. Few colleges hold Saturday classes, so you won't get much chance to sit in on courses or see the bustling life of the college. On Saturday and Sunday mornings a college campus more resembles a deserted park than a lively community of scholars because most students, except for a few in the library, are spending those early weekend hours in a favorite pastime— sleeping.

Don't plan to go Thanksgiving weekend or Christmas week when colleges are closed. Admissions staff may also restrict visits from the application deadline date through April when they are poring over their current crop of applications.

Keep in mind that it is one thing to see a campus on a summer's day when a mere handful of students wander around and only the admissions office is open, and quite another to see the full college in action. But if you can visit campuses only during the summer, here are a few things you can do:

☐ Get acquainted with the admissions staff

☐ Pick up the course catalog and other materials

☐ Talk to whoever is around

☐ Stroll around the campus

Such a visit could be a good beginning for sophomores to gather impressions, but for seniors it is clearly a pale substitute for a visit when classes are in session and all the students are on campus.

It is always best to check your schedule with the admissions office before you get too far into planning.

Traveling Partners

"It'll be a lark," Ted announced to his best friend. "Scott's up at Colgate, and then we'll stay with Lisa at Hamilton and go on to Syracuse and Cornell. We'll have a ball. Especially if we can get some other guys to go along and share the gas." The plan might have worked out except for one thing: None of the boys could convince their parents that it was a good idea. Their parents correctly questioned the usefulness of a trip based mainly on having a good time.

Friends

Making campus visits with friends is a fine way to see colleges, but only if several conditions are met. First, don't look at the trip as a lark or a ball; it is a major undertaking and having fun is only a minor consideration. Second, it takes planning and research to bring it off. If you want your parents' approval, you should present them with specific plans and a well-thought-out itinerary. That will help them to see the journey as a college shopping trip rather than a wild and woolly week's waste.

Going with friends has merit if the itinerary of colleges interests the whole group. Anne, for example, wanted to visit Wooster and Denison in Ohio and her best friend was interested in the University of the South and Vanderbilt in Tennessee. There was no practical reason for these two to journey together. To make going with friends worthwhile it is essential for you to agree on purpose and destination.

The thought of traveling alone to Northwestern and the University of Chicago gave Nina butterflies in her stomach. She had never flown alone before, and the thought of trying to get around in a strange city scared her. Her parents thought it would be better to make the trip with someone else, but no one Nina knew was interested. To solve this problem, Nina put a notice on the guidance office bulletin board and found another senior who wanted to make the same journey. Nina's parents also suggested that she call the admissions staff, who proved most helpful by sending her directions and setting up a host to stay with on campus.

Groups

There are other partners to team up with to make campus visits. Some colleges, among them Oberlin and Mount Holyoke, sponsor trips from metropolitan areas for in-depth two-day visits. There are independent businesses that take students on exploratory tours. Enthusiastic parents sometimes drive a caravan of students to a group of colleges. Some colleges, like Amherst, invite alumni children to attend a special meeting with admissions staff. Frequently the school band, choral group, or Model U.N. club will visit an area rich in colleges. Students should take advantage of any of these opportunities whenever feasible.

Some colleges—Trinity University in Texas is one—invite groups of prospective candidates to experience a campus weekend set up to include a campus tour, classes, interview opportunities, overnight in dorms, admission sessions, and a chance to meet faculty and students. Others have informational open houses with one-day or afternoon programs.

Parents

Students often wonder if their parents should go along on campus visits. There are, indeed, advantages to their presence. Parents may lend both emotional and financial support for the venture, and sometimes a more objective view. It is certainly a lot easier to manage a complicated driving schedule with the aid of parents. While your parents do the worrying about arriving on time, you can relax and enjoy the scenery.

When you are interviewing with the admissions counselor, your parents can talk with the financial aid officer, or they can walk around the campus and gather impressions to compare later. Parents can play Dr. Watson to your Sherlock Holmes, all of you picking up clues that help determine if the college is a good match. Moreover, admissions counselors are generally pleased to meet parents *after* the interview and answer any questions they may have. When parents go, they should arrange to stay in nearby lodging while you stay overnight on campus.

Cora certainly appreciated having her mother along. With two sisters and one brother, it wasn't often that Cora had her mother all to herself. The long ride from Virginia to colleges in Pennsylvania gave Cora a chance to tell her mother all about her plans and hopes for college. She found that her mother's good humor and reassuring perceptions helped ease her tension about the upcoming interviews. When interview time arrived, her mother quietly left to investigate the library and later told Cora what she had discovered. After Cora's interview, her mother had a chance to ask the counselor her questions about the college.

Of course, you know how well you travel with your own parents. Some young people feel that their parents will take control of the visit and influence their reactions to a college. For others, parents' enthusiasms set off a negative reaction and the students take an instant dislike to what their parents admire. If you have these kinds of concerns, it's a good idea to air them with your parents before planning a campus visit.

Alone

For some students, visiting colleges alone is the first act in the drama of "going away to college." There's a sense of freedom and a spirit of adventure implicit in the journey. For Connie it meant seeing a campus through her own "I's" only. Even though her parents' and her friends' opinions were important to her, Connie decided that her college tours were better done alone. She thought it would be easier to have casual conversations with lots of students and tour the campus at her own pace without having a friend or her parents waiting around. She knew she would reflect better on all she had seen if she had time to herself to size things up.

Checklist for Going

Go	**Advantages**
☐ In fall, winter, early spring of senior year	Colleges are in session
☐ On weekdays	Students are available, classes are meeting
☐ When admissions staff welcomes visit	Good reception
☐ During high school holidays, late summer of junior year	You won't miss school

Travel	**Advantages**
☐ With friends	Share experiences, compare notes, companionship
☐ With groups	Prearranged by leader, group input
☐ With parents	Emotional and financial support, second opinion
☐ Alone	Adventure, independent look, freedom

Don't Go	**Disadvantages**
☐ When college is not in session	Campus is deserted
☐ During reading period or exams	Students are busy
☐ On weekends	Limited academic activity
☐ When admissions office is closed for interviews	Counselors unavailable

Selecting Colleges to Visit

Jeff, a varsity tennis player and fledgling photographer for his high school newspaper, was an average student with a solid college preparatory program, some honors courses in history, and junior-year test scores above the national average. He thought he had excellent chances of getting into his state university, perhaps even the honors program, but he wanted other options as well. During the winter of his junior year, Jeff thought about himself and the kind of college he wanted, and certain priorities became clear. He realized that friendships were important to him and he wanted to meet lively people from different parts of the country. He wanted a challenging education, both from classes and classmates, but did not want to be at the bottom of the group. He also wanted to play tennis, do some sports photography, and perhaps join a fraternity. Like most high school students, he wasn't at all sure what he wanted to major in, but he had liked his history courses a lot so he thought that colleges with a strong history department would be good for starters. He still didn't know if a small college or a large university would better suit him. Jeff read some college guidebooks, sent away for catalogs and general information, and in the spring of his junior year sat down with a good map and his college list.

Students must evaluate their academic record, analyze their needs and desires, and research colleges before selecting those worthy of a visit. *Soul-searching* and *researching* are essential elements to determine college preferences. There are various objective, subjective, and specialized guidebooks and directories to aid in the investigation. Check your guidance office, library, and local bookstore. The checklist on page 14 suggests some preliminary criteria for students to apply in narrowing college choices, but students must determine for themselves how each of these fits with their personal priorities.

What Else You Should Do

☐ Write to colleges for current course catalogs. Catalogs are often available in the high school guidance office or the public library.

Preliminary Criteria

Selectivity

Safeties	Possibles	Reaches
_____	_____	_____
_____	_____	_____
_____	_____	_____
_____	_____	_____

Type

Public_____   Private_____   College_____

University_____   Liberal arts_____   Specialized_____

Technical_____   Coed_____   Single-sex_____

Religious_____   Historically black__   Minority_____

Location

Geographical _____

Community: Urban____ Suburban____ Small town____ Rural____

☐ Size _____

☐ Cost _____

☐ Academic courses _____

☐ Special programs _____

☐ Other _____

☐ Familiarize yourself with course catalogs. These are indispensable for a solid knowledge of what colleges offer (see Chapter 6, *How to Read a College Catalog*).

☐ Talk to college students when they're home on vacation (see Chapter 5, *Main Components on Campus*).

☐ Seek help from your school's guidance counselor and your parents.

☐ Attend college fairs and speak to college representatives.

☐ Talk to an expert in your field of interest and get suggestions and advice.

When You Cannot Visit

Julia felt left out of her crowd's college planning. Most of her friends were mapping out trips to colleges in Texas and California, but Julia couldn't go. Responsible for all her personal expenses, Julia worked after school and on weekends, and didn't have the time or money to tour colleges that were far away from home. She worried that without visits she wouldn't learn enough about the colleges to make intelligent choices.

Indeed, there are circumstances that could prevent you from making any campus visits, and there is a limit to the number of colleges you can investigate personally; colleges may be too far away, and money or time may be in short supply. How, then, do you learn enough about colleges to know if you want to apply?

First, as already noted, evaluate your record, do some soul-searching, and research the colleges.

Second, follow through by talking to students, preferably face to face, who are at colleges that interest you. Arrange this by asking your guidance counselor or registrar for the names of students from your high school who are enrolled at these colleges. You may also write to the college admissions office for a list of students who live in your area. If there is a department, sport, or extracurricular activity in which you are particularly interested, ask the admissions office to put you in touch with like-minded students. Have your searching questions ready to ask (see Chapter 5, *Main Components on Campus*).

Third, look at the video or computer presentations of colleges if available in the guidance office, but be aware that the public relations people designing these portrayals often show colleges at their resplendent best.

Fourth, speak to college representatives at the college fair and during their visits to your school. Remember, you are shopping for a college that will best suit your needs, so ask questions!

Fifth, arrange for interviews in your home town, either with alumni or the college representative.

But, after acceptance and before you enroll, make sure you're making the right choice by visiting the college.

Chapter 2

Making Plans

Gauging the Choices

When Jeff sat down with a map to plan his itinerary of campus visits, he had his list of colleges in hand. He had divided them into three categories: "safety" schools, where he thought his chances of being accepted were excellent; "possibles," where he believed his chances were good; and "reaches," where his chances were "iffy." He resolved to study harder during the remainder of his junior and senior years, and hoped to improve his test scores the following fall, both of which would open up his options and strengthen his chances for admission.

His college adviser and his parents helped him evaluate his list. Of a dozen colleges, he had three "safeties," five "possibles," and four "reaches." Everyone agreed this was a good number and distribution for starters. He might add some colleges later, but eventually he would reduce the total number to between six and eight, keeping a similar distribution in the categories. His final list would represent a range of possibilities that guaranteed him a choice of acceptances.

Mapping the Visits

To avoid crisscrossing the same area on different visits, Jeff arranged the colleges into geographic categories. He saw that he had three colleges scattered across New England, two in Pennsylvania, one in New York, four in the Midwest, and his state university and one "safety" close to home. On his counselor's advice, he planned to visit his "safeties" to be sure that given the worst-case scenario he would have at least one college he wanted to attend. One of the "safeties" was in the Midwest where two of his "possibles" and one of his "reaches" were, making a journey there worth taking. As he didn't yet know what size college would be best for him, he included a wide range in his list. He realized that his best chances of playing varsity tennis would be in a small, less athletically competitive college but that he could play intramurals anywhere. He would decide later where that fit into his priorities.

A look at the map showed that three of the Midwestern colleges were located within a 100-mile radius, but the "reach" university was quite a distance away. If he flew first to the city where the "reach" was situated, he could then rent a car and see all four. However, there were a few problems: His parents wouldn't let him rent a car alone; he knew he shouldn't schedule his first interview with a "reach"; and the trip would probably take four days, which might be difficult to arrange. He would have to work out another plan for these college visits.

The other geographic area that had potential was New England, but the colleges were widely scattered, and only by driving could he get to all of them. The two colleges in Pennsylvania were fairly close together and were another possibility. His state university and a small "safety" college were near home, and the New York college stood by itself. Jeff put asterisks next to those colleges where an interview was required or recommended and next to two "reach" schools where he thought his chances would improve with a personal interview on campus. The other two "reaches" had group interviews only, and he put a check next to those.

Safeties	Possibles	Reaches
State U—near home, large	C—Midwest, small*	H—Pa., small √
A—near home, medium	D—Midwest, medium	I—NE, medium √
B—Midwest, small*	E—NY, small*	J—Midwest, large*
	F—NE, small*	K—NE, small*
	G—Pa., medium–large	

Getting There

Jeff discussed the chart with his parents, and together they made some plans. His parents suggested that the family take their vacation by car around Labor Day before high school began. In that way they could help with the driving, and Jeff could visit all the Midwestern colleges. His parents reasoned that four days wouldn't be enough time for Jeff alone to scout four colleges, but by combining a family vacation with the visits, there would be plenty of weekday time at the colleges.

Jeff checked the academic calendar to confirm that the colleges he wanted to visit were going to be in session. He then scheduled his interviews, making sure that his "reaches" came after he had some practice at the other colleges. When all the preliminary arrangements were completed, the family's vacation–campus visit plan looked like this:

Friday p.m.	Leave home.
	Drive to midway point: lake country.
Saturday, Sunday	Loaf, fish
	Check schedule of summer theater in area.
Sunday p.m.	Drive to College 1.
	Jeff overnight on campus; family nearby.
	Check vacation guidebooks for things to see.
Monday, Labor Day	College 1: Jeff's campus tour, lunch, classes, interview.
Monday p.m.	Drive to College 2.
	Jeff overnight on campus; family nearby.
Tuesday	College 2: same program as College 1.
Tuesday p.m.	Drive to College 3.
	Jeff overnight on campus; family nearby.
Wednesday	College 3: same program.
Wednesday p.m.	Drive to College 4.
	Stay overnight on road.
Thursday	College 4: same program.
Thursday p.m.	Jeff overnight on campus; family nearby.
Friday	Start drive home; arrive state park.
Saturday, Sunday	Loaf, fish. Investigate area.
Sunday	Arrive home.
Monday	School begins. Back to work.

The itinerary looked fine to everyone including Jody, Jeff's younger sister, who was a sophomore active in the high school drama club. Jody read up on the places in which they would be stopping and found a number of sights to see and things to do. She made a mental note to look at the theaters on each campus they visited so that she would know a bit more when she began her own college search.

Although the trip had its ups and downs, overall the family judged it a success. It gave Jeff the confidence to plan his autumn New England journey with friends, and Jeff's parents knew he had had enough experience to handle it well—they even lent him the car.

Jeff decided to visit the Pennsylvania colleges later in the fall on his own, knowing that after the trip with his family and another with friends, he would have the know-how to interview at one of his top-rated colleges. Between the first and second semesters of senior year, when he had time off from school, he would visit his state university and the "safety" near home. He elected to wait until he had an acceptance before visiting the lone New York college. Jeff's counselor reminded him to check with his teachers about school absences and to take his transcript along to the interviews in case it was requested.

Using Jeff's experience as a guide, you can draw up a list with specific points to follow. Make sure you arrange your plans efficiently so that you do not visit the same college, or the same area, more than once. You don't want to be like Louise, who never quite got her act together. First she visited colleges on a trip with her family, driving through college campuses without even talking to people. When she returned home, she read about colleges, and whenever one attracted her, she persuaded her father to drive her there to take a look. Once in a while she would arrange an interview in advance. If the interview went well, she then planned on an overnight. In the end she visited some colleges two or three times, crisscrossing the same ground, spending lots of money, and wasting time, not to mention disrupting her and her family's routine. The checklist on the next page will help you organize an efficient trip.

Checklist for Making Plans

☐ Evaluate yourself and your academic record. Get help from your college adviser and your parents.

☐ Think about preliminary criteria and your priorities.

☐ Make a college list that includes "safeties," "possibles," and "reaches."

☐ Star colleges where interviews are required or recommended. These interviews must be arranged well in advance, as appointment schedules fill up early.

☐ Map out your itinerary. Plan for a full school day and overnight at each college whenever feasible. Limit each trip to no more than four colleges so that they don't blur into each other. See Chapter 3, "An Ideal Campus Schedule."

☐ Check that the colleges are in session.

☐ Plan how and with whom you'll go. Make sure everyone agrees on the plan. If driving, take maps and plan each day's stopovers; if flying, know schedules of planes and connecting buses. Some airlines and bus companies have fare specials and unlimited travel options. Admissions staff will often arrange for you to be picked up at the airport.

☐ Keep college visits and school demands in balance.

☐ Arrange for high school absence and plan to make up missed work.

☐ Pack appropriate clothes for the interviews (see Chapter 11, *Planning for the Interview*).

☐ Bring sleeping bag, toiletries, and bath towel for overnight on campus. Take an alarm clock if you have trouble waking up in the morning.

☐ Write names, phone numbers, and dorm of contacts on campus in a small notebook to take with you. Jot down time of interview appointments.

☐ Bring questions. Be sure you have a pen with which to write information and impressions in your notebook. Pack a good book to read in case you get stuck with nothing to do.

☐ Take money for meals and expenses (some colleges give candidates meal vouchers and activities passes).

☐ Bring transcript in case admissions counselor requests it.

Chapter 3

Making Arrangements

Admissions Office Contact

Doug, who realized he would miss having a variety of movies and restaurants near the small town colleges he had first considered, buckled down to his college "homework." He decided to do better research for his next round of college visits. After making a new list of colleges that interested him, he went to the main library and looked up the local newspapers in the cities where those colleges were and wrote to the papers that weren't available in the library, asking for a recent edition. He intended to look at the movie and restaurant ads to get an idea of each city's offerings. He also wrote to the admissions offices, requesting a copy of the college's weekly calendars. He also asked to be sent publications about off-campus events, which were available at some colleges, such as Princeton and Columbia. All this information would tell him much more about the college activities on and off campus.

Nora, a visually impaired senior, also wrote to the admissions offices to make arrangements for her college visits. She asked each office if an escort could be provided to help her on her tour. In addition, she requested that they send her the names of visually impaired students on campus so that she could discuss with them the extent of the support services the colleges offered.

Having been a cheerleader all through high school, Marge was pretty certain she would continue this activity in college. She decided that during her visits she wanted to watch a practice session and talk with the squad. She made arrangements to go in the fall when the groups would be practicing daily.

Another student, Nils, was interested in acting and directing, but he also wanted a good creative writing and English department. This meant investigating college programs where he could get both vigorous drama training and a solid liberal arts program. He knew from a friend's experience that a good way to judge a drama program was to attend student productions. He wrote to colleges requesting performance dates so that he could time his visits accordingly.

Addresses and Phone Numbers

To make a campus visit worthwhile, it is best to contact the admissions office well in advance. Before venturing out, write or call them to make arrangements. The addresses and phone numbers of colleges and universities are in most college guidebooks. Some colleges have toll-free numbers: If you want to see whether a specific college has one, check with AT&T Information (1-800-555-1212).

Although queries may be formally addressed to the director or dean of admissions, most inquiries and appointments are handled by the admissions office secretarial staff, and a student admissions folder is generally begun with the first letter of inquiry. While arrangements made by phone do not usually initiate a file, phone calls may be more convenient and allow for better coordination if there are several colleges to be visited on one trip. You should ask the admissions office to confirm telephone arrangements in writing, so everyone has the signals straight.

Jeff's letter (next page) to the admissions office of the college he planned to visit alone in the fall could be a model for one of your letters.

Sample Letter

450 Marshall Road
Endicott, MD 21048
June 24, 19—

Dear Dean of Admissions:

   I am interested in visiting Burgess College and
having an interview during my school holiday, September 15-18. I would like to arrive on campus in
time to take an afternoon tour, and I would therefore appreciate having a schedule of the tour
times. If at all possible, I would appreciate an
interview on the day following my arrival as I
would like to talk to students, visit some classes,
and stay overnight before meeting with the admissions staff. I would also like to have an opportunity to speak with a history department faculty
member and the tennis coach if that could be arranged.

   To prepare me for my visit, would you kindly
send me your current course catalog, any brochures
on special programs associated with the study of
history, your athletics brochure, a copy of the
campus newspaper, and your application. I would
also like the names of any Burgess students living
in my area so that I can talk to them during the
summer.

   Thank you for your assistance.

Sincerely yours,

Jeffrey Miller

Checklist for Arrangements

☐ Arrange an interview appointment. Note the day and hour, and, whenever possible, the name of your interviewer. Book your appointment far in advance, as admissions officers fill their appointment schedules early.

☐ Plan to stay overnight on campus. If you have a special interest, ask the admissions office to arrange for a host with similar tastes.

☐ When possible, ask to stay with sophomores since they usually have enough experience to give you the range of information you want and are still close to you in age.

☐ Plan to attend some classes that interest you. Get the course schedule from the admissions staff for classes in a subject you're interested in. Ask if there will be a schedule handy when you arrive.

☐ Arrange to speak to faculty or coaches or to attend a particular event in a field of interest.

An Ideal Campus Schedule

If possible, arrange your visit so that the interview is one of the last items on your schedule. This will give you ample time to gather impressions and information that will increase the value of the interview. An ideal pattern for a campus visit is as follows:

1. Arrive on campus in the afternoon.
2. Take a late-afternoon guided tour.
3. Have dinner and stay overnight with host.
4. Attend a social, cultural, athletic, or special event.
5. Next morning, attend classes and walk around campus.

6. Talk to faculty in subject of interest; see coaches.
7. Eat lunch and talk with students.
8. Have interview.
9. Take a breather and make some notes.
10. Leave campus for next college on itinerary.

Chapter 4

In the Admissions Office and Around Campus

When Connie arrived at the campus, let's call it Burgess College, she was a little on edge. Even though she had read up on the college, studied the course catalog, and talked to a friend who went there, she was still anxious about her visit. The admissions people had been cordial on the phone when she arranged for the visit and interview, but she was leery about meeting a bunch of strangers who could decide her fate. She also wasn't sure what she should do first. If you are feeling as uneasy as Connie, don't worry. You'll be surprised at how welcoming the admissions staff is.

The first thing to do on arriving on campus is to check in with the admissions office. The staff consists of the office personnel and the admissions officers, headed by the dean or director of admissions. Admissions staff see their job as a link between students and the college. They are there to welcome potential applicants and help them learn about the college.

Student and staff have a mutual interest: finding out if the college and the candidate make a good match. Providing prospective applicants with information is a major facet of the staff's work; meeting candidates and sharing their enthusiasm and knowledge with them is a favorite part of their job. Although the admissions officers conduct the interviews and read the applications, their job at this point is to help candidates determine if the college is a good choice.

Connie's job was to be a competent and responsible college shopper. As yet she didn't know if she even wanted to apply to Burgess. She was visiting to pick up clues that would answer her question, "Is this a good match for me?" From the moment she set foot on campus, Connie had to be alert to all aspects of the college. At the end of her exploratory visit she would evaluate what she had seen and experienced, and only then would she decide if the college met her criteria for applying.

A Day on Campus

Connie started her detective work in the admissions office, where she collected material on departments and special programs and picked up an extra application blank just in case she made a mistake on the one she already had. To zero in on the ambience of the college, she picked up the school newspaper, the calendar of weekly events, the class schedule, a campus map, and that gold mine of information, the course catalog.

The school newspaper gave Connie a view of the news on campus and the issues that concerned students. The paper also contained sports pages, ads for snack places, notices of coming events, and personals. The calendar of weekly events told her whether there were concerts, plays, movies, sports events, dances, or special lectures on campus. Connie looked at the newspaper and calendar immediately, then tucked them away to take home and review at her leisure.

Connie also looked over the Burgess yearbook and noticed that the students looked cheerful, spirited, and alike: The men had short haircuts and the women wore conservative tailored clothes. Most of the featured activities seemed fraternity or sorority related. Connie wasn't sure if that represented the majority outlook on campus, so she jotted down a note to ask students about it. The student guide arrived and was warmly greeted by the staff. Connie thought he seemed outgoing and good natured and wondered if this were true of everyone on campus. The office had an air of affability that was hard to resist, and Connie felt her tension draining away.

The small group of prospective applicants and some parents gathered in the admissions office. The two other young women, one with a friendly, easygoing parent, seemed fairly relaxed. There was a pleasant-looking fellow who was traveling by himself. The other young man, with parents who kept nagging him, looked as if he'd rather be elsewhere.

Connie felt comfortable with this group as they followed the guide around the campus. She took particular notice of the bulletin boards and posters. There were notes tacked on the boards from students who came from all parts of the country offering rides home over the autumn break. There were rides to lots of places in New England, New York, and New Jersey, and, to Connie's surprise, there also were queries asking for transportation to places west of the Mississippi and down South, which indicated a lot of geographic variety. One poster announced a poetry reading by a famous writer-in-residence, another reminded members of a meeting of the gay–lesbian group, another invited students to a gathering for vegetarians, and yet another listed the schedule of the film society. "Wow! This place has it all," thought Connie. "But does anyone here ever study?"

On the one-hour tour, the guide enthusiastically answered questions and told a number of lively stories about the college. The group tramped by and through the old and new libraries, the science labs, the gym, the theater and arts center, and the pride of the college, the new student center, which contained several snack areas, meeting rooms, a game room, an auditorium, and the student mail room. Crowded with students, it obviously was a prime gathering place. Connie noticed that these students didn't have the uniform look that characterized the students in the yearbook. Bearded fellows wearing jeans and hiking boots sat next to clean-cut guys in cords and crewneck sweaters; some women wore casual pants and blouses, some were elegantly color-coordinated, and some were dressed in punk style. "Anything goes," thought Connie, deciding that the Burgess campus seemed to have lots of diversity.

After the tour, Connie followed a friend's advice: "Get lost," the sage sophomore had told her. "That's the best way to really find out what a place is like." With the campus map for security,

Checklist for Admissions Office and Tour

Pick up:

- ☐ Course catalog
- ☐ Calendar of weekly events
- ☐ College newspaper
- ☐ Brochures on special programs
- ☐ Class schedule
- ☐ Campus map
- ☐ Extra application forms
- ☐ Host's name and dorm: where to meet

Look at:

- ☐ Yearbook
- ☐ People in office, people on tour
- ☐ Students
- ☐ Bulletin boards, posters all over campus

Make sure you have time to:

- ☐ Have an interview
- ☐ Take a tour

Connie knew she would eventually find her way to her host's dorm. She wandered around the tree-lined, sunlit campus trying to imagine how it might look on a dreary, rainy day. She explored places the guide hadn't covered, getting directions from some students, talking at greater length with others, and all the time asking questions. She found the students helpful and friendly, and she savored her "lost" status.

Connie particularly wanted to investigate the psychology department. She had enjoyed psych in high school and thought she might like to explore the subject further in college. The following day she had an appointment with a psychology fac-

- [ ] Eat a meal
- [ ] Talk to students
- [ ] Meet faculty/coaches
- [ ] Attend a social, athletic, cultural, or political event
- [ ] Talk to students in academic or recreational area of interest
- [ ] Stay overnight in a dorm

Keep in mind:

- [ ] The sunshine factor: A beautiful sunny day can be seductive; a rainy day can dampen you and your interest. Try not to let the weather affect your judgment.

- [ ] Campus guides are not all alike: Some are lively, interesting students who are reliable spokespersons for the school; others may not be well rounded or informed. Don't judge a school solely by the one student tour guide. Meet lots of other students to get a true picture.

- [ ] No single person represents an entire college: Most admissions people and faculty are helpful, but here and there one may be having a hard day. Don't be put off by one person who seems impatient with your questions.

ulty member, but for now she wanted to wander around and meet some psych majors and find out as much as she could about the department. Getting directions from a pleasant student who welcomed her to "this goofy place," she walked into the psych building. On the bulletin boards were several requests for student volunteers for experiments in learning theory, and Connie made a mental note to ask the professor about the project. She saw that the departmental library was packed with students. People *did* study here!

Leaving the psych building, Connie walked across the campus to her host's dorm, noting that it was a good 10 minutes' walk away. As she opened the main door, music surged out from all sides. The loud music and lively conversations among students in the hallways appealed to her. On every door was a chalkboard with messages. Someone introduced herself and directed Connie to her host's room.

Sue, a Burgess sophomore who hadn't yet decided on a major because she was fascinated by just about every course she had taken, was waiting for Connie. She wanted to have an early dinner because later in the evening she was chairing a meeting on the lack of adequate night lighting on campus. She invited Connie to attend the meeting but also told her that there was a special lecture on stream ecology by a visiting zoologist, a square dance, and a movie to choose from that night. Connie also learned that the main library stayed open until 2 a.m. and that there was a room for "all-nighters." "Awesome," thought Connie.

The two rushed through dinner in the dining hall, gabbing with Sue's friends who were all keyed up about the coming meeting and were already drafting a letter to submit to the administration. Connie didn't much like the watery lasagna and thought the pudding tasted like sweet glue, and she gathered that the dinner was pretty much par for the course. Food didn't seem to occupy the students' thoughts as much as the proposal they were framing. After dinner Sue and Connie parted, arranging to meet back at the dorm later.

A friend of Sue's from lit class took Connie in tow to the square dance. At the dance, conducted by a student caller with tapes, Connie ran into Jeff, the pleasant fellow from the guided tour. Greeting each other like old friends, they compared notes on their day on campus and agreed to meet after their interviews the following day to tell each other how things had gone. It was a great end to an interesting and fulfilling day. Both had prepared well for their visit.

The preceding checklist shows the features that Connie and Jeff covered to make their day worthwhile. You should do the same.

Chapter 5

Main Components on Campus

Connie's and Jeff's college visits didn't end with the official tour and the overnight, for they planned to cover acres of campus territory the following day in addition to having their interview. Their goal was to explore the many facets of the college rather than merely look at buildings or judge the beauty of the campus. They wanted to find out what the college offered and whether it suited them. It was a serious undertaking, but each had a plan.

Since a college campus is a complex place to investigate, it helps to have a system. One way to accomplish your tasks is to *divide your campus exploration into five areas*:

1. The students
2. Social life and campus activities
3. Campus facilities
4. The community outside the campus
5. The academic courses and faculty

Start with the student body to determine what kinds of students attend the college.

The Students

Friendships are an important part of your life in college. You will be learning almost as much from your close friends and classmates as from your professors and books. It is therefore crucial to get a clear picture of the students on each campus. You will have to decide if students are friendly, interesting, pleasant, smart. You must determine their academic attitudes, detect their social styles, discover their interests and enthusiasms, and discern their backgrounds and goals.

Not exactly a piece of cake, but scouting for facts, analyzing your observations, and heeding your reactions are your tools in this important quest. You're bound to base some conclusions on mere impressions, but if you keep your eyes and ears open, and collect clues like Sherlock Holmes, your time on campus will be well spent.

Academic Attitudes

In assessing students' academic attitudes, you should evaluate their approach to college studies and intellectual pursuits. Get a feeling for how genuinely involved they are in their studies. Is learning an essential element of their college life? Ask students what the academic pressure and work load are like and how many hours a week they study. Do they seem bright? Are they alert and involved? Are they apathetic or drab? Is the college loaded with superior, average, or below-average students? Will you be able to compete easily or with difficulty? Will you shine or be eclipsed? Jeff liked the idea of demanding studies, but he didn't want to spend all his time hitting the books. Connie, on the other hand, worked better in an environment where she would be challenged by the abilities of her classmates. Marge, another campus visitor, wanted a relaxed atmosphere where she could spend time on homework and term papers without sacrificing her social life and good times. Does the academic approach of the students match *your* idea of a college education? How would you fit in academically?

Social Styles

To determine the social styles of the students on campus, weigh their ways of having fun. Is there an appropriate balance between studies and good times? Do people work hard and play hard? What is the stand on the three D's: drinking, drugs, and dating? Is there an identifiable "in" group? Is there a big rah-rah spirit on football weekends? Are fraternity parties the scene? Do students generally pair off, or do they do things in groups?

Investigate whether there are a variety of activities that provide social vitality. Find out if a good number of students participate in clubs and extracurriculars. Marge wanted to be with students who shared her eagerness for the big college weekend, while Connie preferred people who liked movies and good conversation. Both talked to students to find out if the social style suited them.

Interests and Enthusiasms

Discover what it is that really motivates and excites the students. Do you get a sense of a fervent intellectual exchange of ideas or one of bored passivity? Do students flock to the movies, theater, concerts, and art lectures? What is the focus of the school spirit? Is the talk centered on the opposite sex, the opposing teams, or opposition politics? Are students bent on preparing for careers, are they thinking about job offers and salaries, or are they looking for "alternative" lifestyles? Learn whether students share your interests or have others that might prove stimulating.

Backgrounds and Goals

There should be enough students on campus whose backgrounds are similar to yours to make finding friends easier. For example, Frank wanted enough black students at his college to ensure a community of interest, and Josh wanted to participate in an active Hillel social life. Church activities were important to Karen, so she wanted to meet students who shared her religious values. Idealistic Warren didn't want to be left out in the cold without some soulmates. Marge, who had never been out of her small town in the Midwest, longed to test her wings somewhere else but wanted some familiar types around for support. Ask questions to confirm that there are enough students like you on campus.

However, you also want to branch out and meet people with different backgrounds and outlooks. Find out if there is a sizable contingent that hails from various parts of the country and the world. Do the students represent a variety of geographic, economic, religious, ethnic, and racial environments? Is there enough diversity on campus to ensure a good mix? Most important, are these people with whom you can become good friends?

Appearances

Pick up clues from students' appearances to help in your evaluation. Notice whether the students all tend to look alike. Do they dress much the same as you do, or the way you'd like to dress? Do they look the way you want to look in college?

Clothes and hairstyle are sometimes pretty good indicators of personal style. On each campus Jeff visited, he compiled a "shoe review" by taking a rough count of how many students were wearing the same brand of sneakers or the same color and style of loafers or hiking boots or the same trendy shoe. He figured that lots of duplication indicated a follow-the-leader mentality and little individuality.

Similarly, you can take a survey to see if people are wearing identical shirts with the collars turned up, or if the majority of eyeglasses are horn-rims or wire frames. Are students dressed in the latest fashion craze? Are they into sixties camp or new-wave expensive? Do look-alikes predominate, or is there a variety of styles of dress and haircuts? Are there overcoats and down jackets, jeans and cords, skirts and slacks, button-downs and flannel shirts, bushy heads and crew cuts? Does one look prevail, such as jock or preppy, country or city, casual or dressy?

Conversations

Careful observation will bring in quality returns. Choose a spot to watch the passing parade, and listen to the conversations going on around you to capture the campus mood. What students are thinking and talking about tells you a lot about the vitality of the campus.

Some vantage points are the student center, any eatery,

the library lounge, the bookstore, and the mail room. What are students discussing, what are their gripes? Get some impressions from their conversational styles. Is the vocabulary smart-alecky or trendy or deadpan? Do they speak in preppy lockjaw or in street talk? Are they animated or groggy? Do they look terminally happy? What is the nerd factor? Are they discussing the merits of their courses or their cars? Are they talking politics or parties? Connie listened in on a group of students who were lolling on the grass debating the merits of the foreign film series playing at the student center, and knew she had found kindred spirits.

Books and Bulletin Boards

Since books are the basics of college, notice which ones students are carrying. Are they reading Ludlum and Buscaglia or Braudel and Bloom? What magazines and newspapers are in the bookstore racks: *The Village Voice* and *People*? *The Nation* and the *National Review*? Unfamiliar magazines as well as well-known popular ones?

Get an idea of campus doings by checking out the numerous bulletin boards and posters. Are there notices for different religious clubs? Is there a black, Hispanic, Asian, or Native American student meeting scheduled? Is a feminist group holding a discussion? Is there a political action planned? Is there an eating disorders meeting? Are the requests for rides home to mostly local places? Also notice what students advertise for sale—motorcycles or three-speed bikes, software or texts?

Free Time

Get an idea of what students do in their free time. Are they involved in activities that provide opportunities to expand themselves outside of studies? Are they potting, puttering, or practicing? Are they in the student center playing chess, pinball, or pool? Talking together or watching a soap opera? Playing soccer or frisbee?

By making extensive, personal observations while on campus, and by talking with many students, you will get a better notion of what kinds of students attend the college. You will know more about their attitudes, their study habits and interests, their backgrounds, social styles, and behavior. Think over what you've observed. Would you like to spend four years with such students? Would you enjoy being their friend?

Social Life and Campus Activities

You won't be occupied with studies 24 hours a day, so social life and activities become an important part of your college experience. Cast your line and fish for clues on this aspect of campus life.

The best way to get responses to your questions is to chat with as many students as possible. College students like to talk about their experiences, and they have a yard of opinions about their college. Connie's opening gambit was, "I'm thinking of applying to Burgess, but I'd like to know more about the social life." Jeff said, "I don't know anything about fraternities. Can you describe them?"

The big social question is, *What do students do for fun?* What happens on weekends? Do students enjoy doing things on campus, or do many leave for greener pastures? Are there major campus events, such as a winter carnival or a spring fling, that everyone attends? What is weekend social life like at a single-sex college?

Fraternity and Sorority Life

Fraternities and sororities provide a readily available group of friends, social life, and often housing for their members. The white pillared mansions on and around campus are often home to the Greek letter societies. Talk to sorority sisters and fraternity brothers to find out what the main activities of the group are and what it takes to join. Ask if fraternities play an active role in the social life of the majority of students, or whether they are one of several social choices on campus. Investigate whether the college administration has imposed limitations on pledging and rushing or on hazing and initiation rites. What impact has this had? If you wouldn't want to join a fraternity or sorority, ask other students if you would still have lots of other social options.

Other Social Groups

Find out if there are particular groups on campus around which social life revolves. Are these groups formal or informal? Do they interact with one another, or does one group dominate life on campus? Are there cliques? Is it possible not to join and still have a busy life? *Don't hesitate to ask.*

Parties and the Three D's

What about campus parties? Who throws them? Who goes? How often and how rowdy? Are they straight out of *Revenge of the Nerds* and *Animal House*? When was the last toga party?

What is the predominant view on drinking, drugs, and dating? Is there pressure to conform? Does the administration have rules and regulations regarding social activities? Do you detect evidence of special problems, perhaps from a newspaper story or whispers in the corridors? Connie found that one of the advantages of staying overnight in the dorm was that these hard questions were easier to ask when she shared a midnight snack with her host and her friends.

Clubs and Activities

Find out if there are clubs organized around special interests and hobbies, such as politics, rock climbing, religion, singing, or intramural sports. Do any clubs sponsor campus-wide events? Are there signs of an active student government? Are there cultural activities such as movies, concerts, plays, or art exhibits? Liz, who wanted to join the band, watched a rehearsal and spoke to other brass players to get the scoop on the conductor. Are there clubs and activities related to your interests?

Read several issues of the calendar of weekly events and see what activities are promoted. Investigate whether the activities are well balanced and supported by the administration and the students. What are the big sports on campus, and how much school spirit do the games arouse? Is everyone into football weekends, or are there other noteworthy activities going on even during the big game?

Connect with what you hear, see, and read. There is luck

involved in meeting people who will give you an accurate and balanced view of the college, but if you *talk to lots of students who represent a cross-section of interests*, you will get a pretty realistic picture. Walk around. Look around. Take your time. What vibes are you picking up?

Campus Facilities

The guide who escorted Connie and Jeff on the official campus tour took his group into many of the buildings, but some guides may merely point out from afar the gym or the theater or the dorms. To get an authentic sense of the campus facilities, it is advisable to explore areas not covered on the tour. Connie "got lost" and found that a great way to scout around.

Housing

A good place to start is the dorms. There are many varieties of housing arrangements at colleges. Buildings may be one or more stories or even high-rise; they may be clustered or spread all over the campus. Housing may be coed or single-sex, or the sexes may be separated by floor. There could be a choice of a single or double room or a suite shared by three or four. There may be dorms for freshmen only with assigned roommates or dorms where all the classes live together and the choices are yours. Find out if there is on-campus housing for all four years or if there is a problem with overcrowding.

In addition, there may be special-interest dorms, such as a French house where only French is spoken or a co-op house where food expenses and activities are shared. You may find all the campus athletes live in the same dorm. Some dorms may be so noisy that you'll need a refuge for quiet study.

At some colleges, there may be a residential college system in which students live in independent facilities, provided with their own dining halls and special activities, under the supervision of a house master. Find out what your housing options are on each campus.

Investigate the living quarters and see if there is space to move around in; if the furniture is built in, nailed down, or movable; if there are enough closets and showers. Is there a snack area in the building or a refrigerator handy? Do students have small cooking appliances in their rooms? See if the common areas are attractive and well kept. Where are the laundry facilities? College housing will seldom match the comforts of home, and you should get an idea of the pleasures or discomforts that await you.

Dining

Another area of more than passing interest is the dining halls. Eat a meal whenever you can, but remember that no restaurant guide ever raved about college food. Find out what dining facilities there are, such as snack bars, coffee houses, or cafeterias. Are there unlimited servings and a variety of options such as vegetarian, low calorie, or kosher food?

Dining is more than eating, though. Many students linger long after the meal is over to socialize, so this is a good place to find the answers to your questions and listen to the conversations going on around you. Nils got the inside story on the drama department while munching on a hamburger, and Jeff discussed the strengths of the history department in the bagel den.

Note also how far dining facilities are from the dorms. If it were snowing or pouring rain, what would it be like to go from bed to board?

Activity Centers

State universities, large private universities, and some small colleges often have a student union or student center that houses many extracurricular activities. In addition to eateries and lounges, there may be club and game areas, a music room, a meeting hall, and theaters. Smaller colleges may not hold all their activities in one building, so look for the location on campus of those facilities that interest you.

The student center, usually run with student participation, is where people get together for after-hours fun. It can contribute to the "good life" on campus and is often the hub of student activities. Check out the student center to see if its ambience appeals to you.

Athletic Facilities

Most colleges have extensive sports facilities. Notice if the gym is open at all times to everyone or if varsity sports have priority ranking. Can you play squash or racket ball whenever you want? Is there an indoor track and pool? Connie asked if the pool was open to lap swimmers at particular hours; Jeff counted the tennis courts. Does the college have a crew team? What share of the facilities are for women's sports?

The college should have varying levels of activity to accommodate interested students of different abilities so that no one is eliminated because the level is too high or too low. This is important not only in sports but in all other recreational activities as well. Connie thought it would be fun to try out for a play, but since she had never acted before she wanted to find an appropriate group for her fledgling effort. She walked into the theater to talk to the group rehearsing for a show to ask about the various groups that put on plays.

Health, Personal Counseling, Career Services

Colleges usually have an infirmary, and a doctor or nurse or both on call. A visiting student named Jim had asthma, and occasionally needed an emergency adrenalin shot. He checked whether the college itself handled special problems, or whether he would have to get outside help.

Is there also a psychologist or personal counseling office? Does it provide services and tackle problems related to the physical and mental health concerns of students? As you might expect, larger universities often offer a wider range of such services than smaller colleges that haven't been faced with as many diverse problems. Look into how students rate the services.

See if there is a career counseling and placement office on campus. Find out if it serves a useful function for students. Does the college encourage job interviews on campus? Does the college also sponsor a program for minority students?

Special Student Services

Special students, such as the hearing and visually impaired, the wheelchair-bound, the learning disabled, should inquire into the services that colleges provide for their particular needs. Is there an office that handles special services, or an organization on campus that is attuned to special needs? Does the college provide readers or adaptive equipment for the visually impaired; is there wheelchair access to all parts of the campus; are there interpreters for the hearing impaired? Does the campus provide supervised housing or private housing off campus? For a listing of books with more detailed information on special needs, consult the appendix.

Miscellaneous

Computers are another facility on campus worth investigating. Does the college provide access to sufficient computer time at an adequate number of terminals? Are computer rooms open day and night? Do students use word processors for term papers? Is there a state-of-the-art facility on campus? Are there plans for modernization? If you are a science student, see if the lab equipment is up to date.

Walk into the campus bookstore and see what is being sold in addition to textbooks. It may carry a full complement of out-of-town newspapers, special-interest magazines, and bestsellers along with the college T-shirts. Does it also have a line of drugstore items and other necessities?

As you amble about the campus, note the layout and the buildings. Do students find it convenient to get from classes to the dining hall and from the library to their dorms? Are the buildings both old and new and in good shape? Is there an architectural style and unity to the campus that's appealing? Are the grounds well kept? Good maintenance is one indication of sufficient funding in the budget for the college's well-being.

Women should check out the security on campus. How are the students and the administration handling problems of night lighting or escort services? Connie's contact with her host made her aware that lighting conditions at Burgess needed attention and that students were actively involved in improving the situation.

Investigate the groups that handle problems between students and the administration. Find out what role students have in decision making. Is the student government an effective voice for the students?

The Library

You will be spending much of your time in the library, so look it over. Is the staff courteous and helpful? What are the hours? Is there a room for "all-nighters"? You can assume that if the library stays open way into the night weekdays *and* weekends and is crawling with students, you are on a hard-working, serious campus.

See if the stacks are open for browsing or closed, which means working with the card catalog. Are students reading in small carrels tucked away in the stacks? What are the physical conditions of the library? Is the main reading room well lit? Is there enough seating, or does the library seem overcrowded? Is it comfortable? Is there also a lounge where students meet between bouts of hard study? Ask if the library is a good place for study *and* research. Are there long lines at the copy machines? See if there are departmental libraries and special collections open to students and if they have current periodicals. Are books by faculty on display? Ask students what their experiences have been. Do they give the library a good rating?

The Community Outside the Campus

Some colleges are like small cities, containing everything you want for a stimulating life; others depend on the community outside the campus to fulfill needs; and still others may not have enough activity on or off campus. Weigh the college and the community activities to decide whether there is a winning combination for you. The liveliness of the college and the surrounding community can be a big factor in your enjoyment of your four college years.

You want to ask, "Is there life outside the campus?" Find out how far away town is and how to get there. Can you walk or will you need your bike or a car? Is there a bus or do students hitch or rely on other students who have cars? What exactly is that community: a couple of streets with college-related stores, a suburban area with a shopping mall, or a booming city?

If you didn't want to go to any events on campus, could you find something to do in town? If the college has a guide to places and activities off campus, pick it up. Buy the local newspaper. Are there restaurants and movie houses; pubs and pizza places; ice cream parlors and McDonald's? Is there a place to dance or listen to music? If you needed a new dress shirt or a new dress, where could you buy it?

Do the students and the town have anything to do with each other? The movie *Breaking Away* depicted a town/gown clash, the "cutters" versus the students. Is there cooperation or friction with the community? Do students and townspeople join together in an antilitter drive or campaign for local politicians? Do students do volunteer work or tutor in the local school? Could you find a decent paying job in the community? Do students stay in the area after graduation?

You should also consider how far the college is from home, how long it will take to make the journey, how much it will cost, and alternative means for getting from home to college. Remember that greater distances sometimes take less time to cover because you fly rather than drive.

Academics and Faculty

The soul of a college is the *quality of its academic courses and faculty*. Before you visit, study the course catalog to learn about the college offerings (see Chapter 6, *How to Read a College Catalog*). When you're on campus you can check out the validity of what you've read and investigate other academic areas.

One feature to examine is the *academic pressure and work load* on each campus. Inquire about the kinds and number of reading assignments and the hours students spend on studies. If you're a bookworm and love the intellectual tussle, you'll have different needs from someone whose life doesn't revolve around studies.

But no matter what your purpose, note if emphasis is on course content or on grades, if classes are small with individual participation, or if most courses are held in large lecture halls with students scribbling notes and doing little talking. If the latter, ask about the general level of small discussions led by teaching assistants, or better yet, sit in on one of these sessions.

The best way to find some of the answers is to *attend a few classes* in subjects in which you have some background and interest. Observe a typical freshman class and an upper-

Checklist for Main Components on Campus

Area to Research	What to Look for	How or Where to Look
Students	Academic attitudes Social styles Interests Backgrounds	Talk to students and listen to their conversations Go to student center Look at bulletin boards Ask admissions counselor
Social Activities	Parties, athletic and cultural events, clubs	Read bulletin boards and posters, calendar of events, newspaper, and yearbook Talk to students Attend events
Campus Facilities		
☐ Housing	Varieties, location	Visit dorms
☐ Dining	Options, quality	Eat at dining hall
☐ Activity centers	Liveliness, range of activities	Go to center
☐ Athletics and rec-reation	Range, hours	Go to gym, pool, etc.

class course. Are students listening avidly, or are they gazing out the windows? Is the professor reading from well-worn notes without looking up from the page, or is he talking to and with the students? Is the instructor interesting to you? Observe if there's interaction between the instructor and the students and whether the students are prepared for class. Do they participate readily, or is the professor pulling teeth to get a response? Do the students sound knowledgeable? Do you get

Area to Research	What to Look for	How or Where to Look
☐ Health and special student services	Usefulness, range, support	Talk to students and counselors, consult the appendix
☐ Miscellaneous	Computer, bookstore, etc.	Look, ask questions
☐ Library	Hours, comfort, lighting, reputation	Visit, talk to students
Community	Activities Shopping Town/gown relations	Go into town Newspaper Ask students and admissions staff
Academics	Quality Pressure, competition Work load Emphasis	Attend classes Talk to students Read catalog
Faculty	Reputation Quality Availability	Read student course guide Attend classes Talk to students

any sense of intellectual excitement? Consider whether you were stimulated by what took place in class. *Would you be comfortable in this setting?*

Inquire whether the college is changing its academic direction or retaining its current policies. Does the curriculum emphasize writing, critical thinking, and reasoning with a stress on values and ethics, or does the college highlight career preparation? Is the college maintaining its academic stan-

Checklist of More Questions to Ask College Students

About the College's Reputation

- ☐ Has the college lived up to expectations?
- ☐ Has anything been a major disappointment?
- ☐ Was anything surprising to you?
- ☐ Is the evaluation in the subjective guides fair, accurate, up-to-date?
- ☐ What is distinctive about the college? What are its strengths? Weaknesses?
- ☐ Are there any particular tensions on campus?
- ☐ Is there anything special I should see before I leave?
- ☐ If you were to do it all over again, would you still choose this college?

About Housing

- ☐ What is the housing system?
- ☐ Is it quiet enough to study in the dorms?
- ☐ Which dorms are good places to live in?

dards? Have enrollments affected budget cuts? Have budget cuts affected enrollments? If so, what has suffered? Will it affect you?

Ask questions about strong and weak departments, popular majors, and what graduates are doing. (See "Checklist of More Questions to Ask College Students," and Chapter 14.)

Another factor is the reputation of the faculty, not only in their scholarly fields, but also as teachers. How do students rate the teaching quality? Have members of the faculty published books lately? In what fields? You may find these books on display in the library or bookstore. Are some professors

About Activities

- ☐ How difficult is it to make the _____ team? (Fill in your sport.)
- ☐ How can I qualify for the newspaper? Orchestra? Choral group? Radio station? Drama group? (Substitute your special interest.)
- ☐ How can I qualify for intramural sports?
- ☐ What were some social or academic issues that concerned students last year? How did the administration react? What was the result?

About Academics and Faculty

- ☐ Are classes taught by professors or by teaching assistants?
- ☐ How many hours a week do students typically study?
- ☐ How easy is it for freshmen to get the classes they want? Sophomores?
- ☐ Are classes for freshmen usually large? For upperclassmen?
- ☐ Is there good rapport with faculty?

especially popular? Are they tough but scholarly, easygoing and real pushovers, witty or spellbinding lecturers?

What departments have outstanding professors? Do the famous professors teach undergrads or only graduate students? Are the best faculty members teaching core courses and freshman seminars? How many full professors are women or minorities, and is anyone shaking the rafters about the percentages? Which are considered weak departments on campus? Are you likely to concentrate in these areas?

Many colleges have student-sponsored and student-written course evaluation guides that rate the courses and the profes-

49

sors. Pick it up if it is available. It is an invaluable insight into students' opinions and experiences.

Covering the Spectrum

By investigating the students, social life, campus facilities, community, and academics, you'll accumulate vital knowledge about the college and its offerings. Then you can determine whether the college matches your personality, interests, and needs.

Take notes as you go along; heed your gut reactions. Remember that although your student host is a rich source of information, you shouldn't rely too heavily on one person. Connie found it helpful to stay with a sophomore who had a year's experience under her belt and had gotten over her freshman fidgets. Jeff stayed with an older junior who had experienced both the highs and lows of college life. But both talked to many people in addition to their hosts to get a balanced view of Burgess. You must aim for the same.

Once you are home you may find yourself filled with the sights and sounds of the college you visited and unsure of how to sort our your impressions. The checklists in this chapter and in Chapter 7 will provide you with a framework to organize your impressions.

Chapter 6

How to Read a College Catalog

The college course catalog is a gold mine of information for the prospective candidate. More than anything else you may read in your college search, it reveals that most precious substance, the academic quality and character of a college.

Catalogs also tell you if the institution is a university or college; public or private; religious, historically black, or minority; coed or single-sex; four year or two; liberal arts or technical. They contain information about the size, location, history, and philosophy of the college, the academic calendar, and the costs. Catalogs acquaint you with the faculty, campus organizations, housing, student government, and academic requirements and procedures. Above all, catalogs contain detailed information about all the academic programs and courses. A wealth of material is at hand if you read a college course catalog carefully and critically.

To begin with, you must first get the college's current course catalog, which may be available at your high school college center or local public library. Since course catalogs cost the colleges a hefty sum of money to produce and mail, admissions offices will not usually send the catalog unless you specifically ask for one. When writing for information and applications, explicitly request a *current* course catalog. Some state and private universities charge several dollars for their catalogs. In any case, make sure you have the latest edition because courses, professors, and even general requirements may change from year to year. To find out exactly what is happening academically at colleges, you must have the most current material.

The catalog's cover design often depicts the college on an enchanting spring day when flowering trees are in bloom and happy students are strolling about serenely. Colleges will try to attract your attention with the best view that its publications department can produce. But you can't tell a book, or a college, by its cover. Nor can you compare colleges by the size and weight of their catalogs. A large university like the University of Washington, with some 20,000 undergraduates, will have a bulkier catalog than Reed College with its enrollment of 1,000. The answers lie inside.

Academic Calendars

Somewhere on the first pages, often on the inside front cover, is the academic calendar of the college, which gives the dates of the start and end of the school term, exam periods, and holidays. The calendar tells you whether the college runs on a semester, quarter, or trimester plan, or variations known as 4–1–4 and block systems. Every calendar system has both advantages and disadvantages. Consider the different terms and decide which fit in better with your plans.

Semester System

The majority of colleges run on a two-semester system of 15 weeks; the fall semester begins late in August and ends before Christmas vacation, and the spring semester begins after the winter break and ends early in May. There may also be the option of a six- or eight-week summer session. The August start enables students to finish the term before the winter holiday so they don't have term papers or finals hanging over their heads during the break. Many college students use their winter vacations to look for summer jobs that often start early in May.

In contrast to this schedule, a few colleges still begin their fall semester in mid-September and end the second semester sometime in June, even though being out of sync with the majority is a disadvantage. Their students take exams after the Christmas holiday, and consequently many spend their vacations writing papers and studying. They finish the school year in June when many summer jobs have already begun.

Quarter System

Some public universities, especially those west of the Mississippi, run on a quarter system. The academic year is divided into four ten-week terms separated by a two- to three-week vacation. Most students attend the fall, winter, and spring terms, and leave time for a summer holiday or job. This schedule permits students to take more courses each year, thus allowing for the option of graduating sooner. One disadvantage to the quarter calendar is that ten weeks may not be long enough to cover a subject in depth, and students complain that finals come too quickly. Another disadvantage is that students don't always register for consecutive quarters, and as a result continuity and friendships may suffer.

Trimester System

A small number of colleges have a trimester calendar that is a variation of the semester system. Because three 15-week sessions are offered each academic year, students can accelerate their studies by attending all three sessions some years.

4–1–4 System

Some small liberal arts colleges, like Williams and Macalester, have elected a 4–1–4 calendar. This system provides for two 12-week terms with four courses in each term, and an interim term in January in which only one course is permitted, sometimes experimental in nature, either on or off campus. Some colleges using this calendar require students to take the January term, others do not.

Block System

The block system, or Colorado Plan (named after Colorado College where it was initiated), divides the year into nine 3½-

week blocks. In this system, each enrolled student takes only one course at a time, which allows for courses to be held on or off campus. The advantage (or disadvantage, depending on a student's nature) is that a student concentrates solely on one subject in each period. A disadvantage in some cases is that there may not be sufficient time to cover or integrate all the material, although courses may be continued into successive blocks.

History, Mission, and Educational Philosophy

The first few pages in the course catalog usually detail the history of a college and tell where it's heading. Many colleges state their philosophy of education in this section, from which you may glean their educational "mission." The mission of one college is to:

> strive to create an atmosphere in which personal and intellectual integrity, honesty, and concern for others are dominant forces. . . . That [honor] code is a way of life at Haverford. . . . We expect our students to contribute responsibly and considerately, individually and collectively, in the task of fashioning new programs that let us achieve our core aims of academic excellence in a humane and stimulating atmosphere.

Other schools provide their own variations on the theme:

> [Baylor] seeks to provide a democratic and Christian atmosphere on the campus and in classrooms and laboratories, whereby students and faculty may work together with inquiring minds in the discovery and propagation of ideas. Students are taught to think for themselves, to develop intellectual curiosity, and to be self-reliant in their search for truth.

> Education at Bennington is an active experience. The curriculum and the course structure are based on "learning by doing." Students take the initiative and responsibility for their own education. They become practitioners, not observers.

> Stanford provides the means for its undergraduates to acquire a liberal education: an education which broadens the student's knowledge and awareness in each of the major areas of human knowledge; significantly deepens it in one or two; and prepares him or her for a lifetime of continual learning in the varied and changing application of knowledge to career and personal life.

The philosophy of education section will tell you if a school is following a traditional path or striving to incorporate innovative programs. You will also be able to assess if a college is scholarly or career oriented, governed by religious principles, or all things to all students.

The Three R's: Rules, Regulations, and Requirements

The catalog also contains information about the rules, regulations, and requirements of the college. For example, the college may have an honor code, a required senior thesis, a housing policy, and special withdrawal procedures.

The catalog not only specifies the admission requirements but also the academic requirements for graduating—what you need to get in and get out. The catalog will specify whether the college has a core curriculum that every student must take; general education requirements or required clusters of related courses; general distribution requirements that perhaps include competency in a foreign language, math, or science; or simply required courses in your major.

A core curriculum, favored for years by colleges such as the University of Chicago, Columbia, and St. John's College, provides a common base of learning that all students share, contributing a special cohesiveness to the college. The course clusters at the University of Pennsylvania and the distribution requirements of Yale and many other colleges also provide a broad guideline for education. The absence of requirements except in one's major, as at Brown, gives students great leeway in course selection.

The academic requirements will also indicate if a college offers opportunities for independent study and is educationally flexible, emphasizes critical thinking and writing, is strengthening its liberal arts programs or computer studies department, or is career oriented.

Special Programs

Many catalogs include descriptions of special programs, tutorials or independent study, study abroad, interdepartmental programs, field study, internships or practicums, or cooperative work-study. There are consortium affiliations such as the Great Lakes Associated Colleges and the Five Colleges in Pioneer Valley, and combined degree programs of liberal arts and medicine (Brown), or liberal arts and engineering (Franklin and Marshall), or liberal arts and forestry (Allegheny). These programs overcome the confines of the campus and add breadth to the course of study.

Some special programs include an artist or writer-in-residence (Wesleyan) or a special lecture series (Columbia). Some colleges have special freshman orientation plans such as Earlham's outdoor session, Bard's critical writing course, or Princeton's preparation program.

Look for the special programs at each college to see if there is something especially appealing to you.

Facilities

Many catalogs describe campus facilities such as dormitories, dining halls, libraries, the gym, theaters, science labs, and the computer center. They may also describe campus activities such as choral groups, the radio station, athletic programs, newspapers, or fraternities. Some catalogs contain the names and home towns of enrolled students and a chart of the geographic distribution of the current student body.

Academic Courses and the Faculty

The most valuable part of the course catalog enumerates and details the academic departments and the courses. Pay particular attention to this vital, indispensable section.

First, see how the courses are organized. Are they arranged in separate divisions, such as the humanities, sciences, and social sciences, or are they listed alphabetically? Skim through the courses to see the range of offerings. Are there courses in fine art, art history, music, theater, dance, and film? What languages are taught? Are there women's studies or Third World courses. What social science courses are offered? Are there accounting, engineering, computer science, and education departments? You may even find areas you never heard of, such as northern studies (Middlebury) or space physics and astronomy (Rice).

Do specific departments, especially those in which you might be interested, show breadth and depth by the number of faculty, the number of courses offered, and the range of subject matter? Does there seem to be a subspecialty in some departments, for example, a concentration of Hungarian or Slavic courses in the European history division?

Scan the requirements for a major in a department of interest. Are the required courses given annually, or are there some years when certain required courses are not offered? The latter might make for scheduling difficulties later on. For instance, if you choose to take your junior year abroad, would you have trouble finishing the required courses when you returned?

Second, do the descriptions of the courses give you a clear idea of content? How are the descriptions worded—as if by a computer or by a real person? Do they list the instructors' names? Are there some courses that sound especially interesting?

Third, count the number of full-time faculty. Do a mere handful of instructors cover a large range of subjects? Because of scheduling, faculty members rarely teach more than two or three courses each semester, and it may mean that a course you want won't be offered when you want it. Notice also if the professors teach from semester to semester and year to year, or if there are asterisks, daggers, and slash marks scattered after their names. These symbols usually signal that the instructors will be away from classes during all or parts of the academic year and that certain courses may not be taught annually.

In the back of the catalog you may find a list of faculty members that includes information about where and when they received their degrees. What percentage have their Ph.D.s? What colleges and universities did they attend? Do the institutions represent a specific section of the country or a mixture of geographical areas? Are these universities renowned in the professors' fields? Is there a preponderance of Ph.D.s from one university? This might indicate a particular emphasis, specialty, or bias in the department. Did a majority of faculty earn their degrees recently, which might mean they are young, or is there a mixture of degree dates, indicating a wide age range?

Fourth, compare departments within the college to see if a particular department has an overwhelming number of faculty members. This might indicate the relative importance of this department in the academic scheme. Is any department underrepresented by faculty numbers, and is this one in which you were hoping to major?

A large number of adjunct faculty members in certain departments such as drama or film might indicate specialists who come from the outside world to teach a distinct craft—theater makeup, for example; in other departments it may indicate a policy of hiring part-time people to keep costs down. Many colleges hire part-time faculty to avoid paying the higher salaries of full-time professors. In some cases, part-time teachers may not have the same dedication to students as full-time faculty, nor be as well integrated into the college's life. Their commitment to the college may not include office hours when they would be available for student conferences.

Your careful reading of the course catalog will add significantly to your knowledge of the college. Jot down questions as you read and take your list on your campus visit. As a result of your catalog investigation, you will be thoroughly prepared to query students, faculty, and your admissions interviewer. (See Chapter 14, *Questions to Ask Your Interviewer.*)

Viewbooks

Unfortunately, colleges often send viewbooks instead of the course catalog. These booklets are generally produced by the publications office of the college or by a public relations team hired by the college to produce handsome reports. Although easier to read than a catalog, they usually show the college at its pictorial best without providing much significant information. The major drawback of viewbooks is that they merely list course names without descriptions and seldom indicate when and how often courses are given or who is teaching them.

If college viewbooks are your only source of academic information, scrutinize them especially carefully. Ask yourself what image the college is attempting to project in its polished pictures. At some point in your college search, you must check to see if that image is a reality or a promotional come-on.

What are the students doing in the pictures—ambling about a sun-drenched campus, coeds arm in arm? What do you know about the actual weather in that part of the country or the male/female ratio? Are there pictures of students working in the library, studying a microscope slide, listening in class? Do the students all look the same? Is there an ethnic or racial mixture portrayed, and can you check out the percentages actually enrolled? The pictures may embody a recruiting technique and desire rather than reality. You must question what the college is trying to tell you about itself and its emphasis, and you must try to find out how accurate the presentation is.

Other sources of information are special publications featuring a particular department or activity. If you write to the college asking for information and state that you're interested in biology or soccer, for example, you may receive a special brochure on that subject describing the courses, career possibilities, or activity.

Whatever else you receive, and whatever else you are told, remember that studying the catalog is one of the most important ways of getting a sense of the academic quality and character of the college.

Chapter 7

Your Campus Evaluation

Colleges are complex institutions. It really isn't possible to know everything about a college after a brief visit, and even students who have been there for several years might have a hard time giving you an accurate character reference for their college. But visits are the best way to gather clues about a college, especially if you investigate in a rational and systematic manner.

Many colleges may seem similar until you look more carefully at individual aspects. The "College Evaluation Checklist" will help you determine the character and distinctiveness of a specific college and be an aid in comparing colleges. In some parts of the list you may be checking more than one item. You can use the categories as a basis for discussion with your parents and friends. Make as many photocopies of the checklist as you need to cover all the colleges you will be visiting.

College Evaluation Checklist

College	Founded _____
	Location _____
	Size _____
Visit	Date _____
	Weather _____
	In session _____
Costs	Tuition _____ Fees _____
	Room/Board _____

Architecture   ____ Gothic ____ Modern

                      ____ Colonial ____ Classical ____ Mixture

Type   ____public ____private ____religious ____4-year

        ____2-year ____college ____university ____liberal arts

        ____specialized ____technical ____coed ____single-sex

        ____historically black ____minority

Calendar   ____semester ____quarter ____trimester ____4–1–4

        ____block ____summer session

Student Body   ____look alike ____diverse ____friendly ____interesting

        ____smart ____preppy ____dressy

        ____outdoorsy ____casual ____sloppy

        ____preprofessional ____rah-rah ____intellectual

        ____grinds ____careerists ____loners ____sproutsy

        ____moderate ____conservative ____liberal ____radical

        other _____

Social Life   ____college sponsored ____student initiated ____clubs

        ____sports oriented ____cultural ____fraternity

        ____sorority ____religious ____ethnic ____racial

        ____political ____wild parties ____mild parties

        ____dances ____dating ____group socializing

        ____drug and alcohol pressures

        problems _____

College Evaluation Checklist
(Continued)

Campus Facilities

Housing ____dorms ____residential colleges ____apartments

____special interest ____fraternity ____sorority

____on campus ____off campus ____singles

____doubles ____suites ____coed ____single-sex

____spacious ____adequate ____crowded ____rundown

____quiet ____noisy ____sociable ____disability access

problems _____

Dining ____dining hall ____cafeteria ____residential college

____snack bars ____coffee houses ____pubs

____special meals ____quality (high, adequate, low)

____quantity (generous, adequate, meager)

____sociable ____open after hours

Recreation and Activities ____team sports ____intramurals ____gym facilities

____athletic clubs ____student center ____music

____drama ____movies ____art ____newspapers

____radio station ____TV station ____games

____minority clubs ____religious clubs

other _____

Services ____health ____counseling ____career ____employment

____tutoring ____special student ____computer

____bookstore ____security

problems _____

Library ____long hours ____weekend hours ____open stacks

____closed stacks ____outstanding ____good

____adequate ____poor ____lounge ____good lighting

____spacious ____special collections ____departmental

College Evaluation Checklist
(Continued)

Community Outside
___far ___near ___easy access ___city ___town
___suburb ___rural ___restaurants ___pubs
___movies ___shopping ___dancing ___music
___theater ___bookstores ___jobs ___conflicts
___cooperation
other _____

Academics
___pressured ___moderate ___relaxed
___stimulating ___bookish ___dull ___huge classes
___large classes ___small classes ___lectures
___discussions___tutorials___seminars
___innovative ___traditional ___career oriented
___core curriculum ___general ed ___clusters
___distributive ___requirements only within major
___language required ___math ___science
___senior thesis
strong departments _____
weak departments _____
popular majors _____

Faculty
___% Ph.D.s ___% part-time faculty
___# women professors ___# minority professors

Popular Professors
___teach freshmen ___teach upperclassmen
teach what courses _____

_____
_____
_____
_____

College Evaluation Checklist
(Continued)

Special Programs
_____interdisciplinary _____independent study
_____study abroad _____internships _____consortium
_____combined degree _____cooperative programs
_____unusual majors _____honors program
_____Phi Beta Kappa _____freshman seminars
_____freshman orientation

Rating
things liked most _____
things liked least _____

Overall Rating
_____superior _____good _____adequate _____disappointing

Other

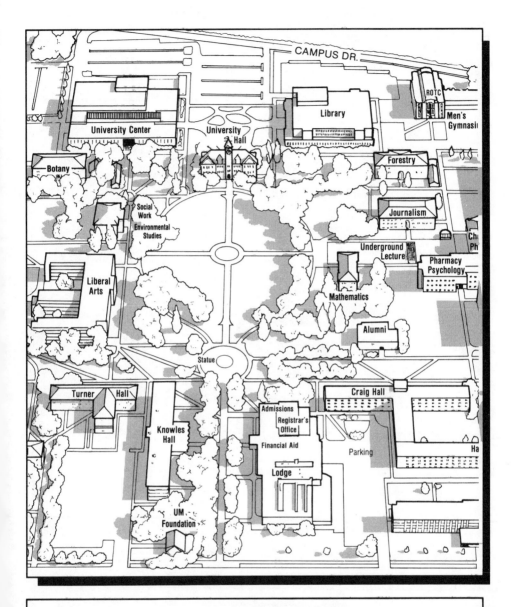

PART 2

The Interview

Chapter 8

Putting the Personal Interview in Perspective

Student Concerns About the Interview

Maggie's hands were shaking as she approached the admissions counselor. She sure didn't like the idea of talking about herself to a complete stranger. Ken's palms were sweaty as he anticipated the third degree. And Doris, who had pitched in any number of softball games without a twinge of nerves, had butterflies in her stomach. These students were suffering from the symptoms of that curable disease, interviewitis.

For many, the interview is the most intimidating part of the whole admissions process. Some students are shy, some are afraid of boasting, some are nervous about not knowing the answers to a barrage of questions. Others think they have to entertain the interviewer with jokes and stories so they won't be asked about their academic record.

One reason for interview anxiety is that most students are not accustomed to talking about themselves, and just the thought makes them uncomfortable. Although students have definite ideas about themselves, they may not have taken the time to organize these impressions into a self-portrait. But if students develop a self-concept as part of their interview preparation, and understand what an interview is all about, they will find their interview jitters fading away. And after a few practice interviews they might even grow to like it. (See Chapter 10, *Putting Your Best Foot Forward*.)

What Is the Personal Interview?

The personal interview is a conversation lasting anywhere from 30 minutes to an hour between two people who share a common purpose. Simply put, it is an *information exchange*. You want to tell the interviewer about yourself, and you want to hear about the college; the interviewer wants to hear about you, and wants to tell you about the college. There is no pass or fail, and it's not the third degree. It's not a rehashing of the transcript, a repeat of the application, or a rerun of the catalog. It is an interchange between two people attempting to explore new ground together.

Why Have an Interview?

One purpose of the interview is to *give yourself an extra boost*. This is the opportunity to show the admissions counselor something nice about you. All during the application process the admissions staff learns about you from a slew of papers: your transcript, test scores, application form. While it is true that you may make a vivid impression in the personal essay and in the recommendations from your teachers and counselor, words on paper can reveal only part of you. In the interview you have the chance to represent yourself directly. Only once during the whole admissions process do you appear as the real, live person you are. That time is in the personal interview.

The interview is your opportunity to talk at some length to an admissions counselor to present a sense of the singular blend of qualities that are yours alone. It's a chance to be your own advocate by talking positively about your interests and enthusiasms.

Laurie, for example, was exuberant and lively. She studied art outside of school and volunteered in a hospice, and her excitement about her work clearly came across in person. Warren had informed opinions on everything from rock music to nuclear disarmament that he was eager to share. Annalee was heavily committed to a complex science project, and Gloria's strength was her ability to work congenially with many different people. Joe was involved in an intricate business enterprise, and Keith was a good all-round athlete. They took the opportunity at the interview to put a face, a portrait, on their written application and be remembered.

The interview is the time to explain a spotty transcript or discuss any extenuating circumstances that affected your studies. Problems that you may find hard to write about in the application are often easier to discuss with a sympathetic admissions counselor. Paul, for instance, had never been a good math student, but this hadn't stopped him from taking advanced math classes. He wanted to tell the interviewer why he had persisted despite the difficulties. When Scott's parents divorced, his academic work took a downturn, and it showed on his record. Lois was dyslexic and needed to make an extra effort with every assignment. Kim's family had moved three times in the past seven years, and each time she had readjusted to a new school and new friends. The interview is a good time to discuss such special situations.

The personal interview will also help you discover the distinctive characteristics of the college not readily found in the catalogs or easily learned from students on campus. The interviewer is qualified to discuss your concerns about the college and answer your queries. (See Chapter 5, *Main Components on Campus*; Chapter 6, *How to Read a College Catalog*; Chapter 14, *Questions to Ask Your Interviewer.*) You will gain more knowledge and a better understanding of the college community, which will help you recognize whether the college is right for you.

How Important Is the Interview?

Most colleges do not require an interview, and therefore do not weigh the interview in their admissions decision; otherwise, they would be rewarding those students who have interviews and penalizing those who do not. At those colleges where the interview is required or recommended (usually small private colleges, highly selective colleges, and nontraditional colleges), the interview is one of *many* factors in the admissions decision.

Typically, interview notes are placed at the end of the applicant's folder, and the admissions committee reads them last. The notes are used to confirm all the other material. "If there is a discrepancy between a teacher recommendation and the interviewer's perception," said one admissions counselor, "we go with the teacher's report. We figure that the teacher knows the candidate much better than we do in our half hour with him."

The Admissions Counselor's View

Although many admissions counselors like students to interview at their college, they admit that the personal interview is not essential, nor is it a key factor in admissions decisions. There is widespread agreement among admissions counselors, however, that a personal interview can work in a student's favor by putting a face on the written application. One admissions counselor explains that the interview can personalize the whole application: "The interview is the occasion for a student to say something pleasant about herself, to confirm the academic record, and to explain something in the record that needs interpretation. The interview can make a difference if you let us know more about you. It's a chance to toot your horn."

All admissions people agree that the "borderline student," the student who is in the "gray area," is most likely to benefit from the one-to-one contact of the interview, especially if the student is willing to speak meaningfully about himself.

Admissions counselors also report that they do not use the interview to weed people out, but to keep people in the running. According to one counselor: "This is no time to be modest. If a candidate mumbles only 'Yes' or 'No' and doesn't make an effort to have some input, then the interview is probably a bust and isn't going to help." If you think you might be a "Yes/No" candidate, read Chapter 12, *Tips for the Shy Person.*

The Student's View

From your standpoint, the interview is very important. You should take every opportunity to give yourself a boost and enhance your written application by presenting your special qualities.

In addition, as a college shopper you are looking the college over to see if it is a good match for you. The interview can sharpen your focus by illuminating the character and special qualities of the college. You can use the interview to ask questions about the college and to inform yourself of factors not covered in the catalog. To discover if a college is one you should apply to, questions are the order of the day, and the interview is one opportunity to get the answers.

More from the Admissions
Counselor's Desk

The admissions counselor has two purposes in the interview. First, to get to know you better; and second, to get you to know the college better. Most interviewers are skilled at getting students to relax, which makes the meeting easier.

Counselors do admit, however, that their best conversations have been with students who come prepared, "students who know something about the college and are ready to talk." As one counselor said, "Don't blow it by asking, 'How many students are there here?' or, 'Do you have an English major?' or, as one student did, 'Say, what college is this?' The well-informed, articulate person can really give herself a lift with a personal interview."

But the admissions officer also knows that you are still a teenager and doesn't expect you to have fully formed goals, ideals, and accomplishments. In wanting to know you better, the interviewer is looking for reasons to accept you, and your job is to provide them. (See Chapter 10, *Putting Your Best Foot Forward* and Chapter 11, *Planning for the Interview*.)

To get you to know the college better, the admissions counselor will talk about the college's strengths (and if you push a little, the weaknesses). Most admissions people regard the interview as a chance to give the candidate their personal view of the college, although they may differ somewhat on what this means. "The real value of the interview," says one admissions counselor, "is that the student can try the college on for size, and the counselor can do good public relations for the college." But another counselor felt less strongly about the promotional aspect: "My role is as an adviser, not a salesperson. I want to tell the student about the college and help him or her make an honest decision."

When the admissions counselor answers your questions and tells you about the college, *listen*. Give the interviewer your full attention. Don't jump from one question to another without waiting to hear the response. Nothing turns an interviewer off quite as much as the student who is merely showing off and only asking questions for effect.

Sometimes the interviewer will also counsel you. If there are indications during the conversation that the college will not work in your best interest, the counselor may suggest other colleges that would. On the other hand, even though admissions counselors do not ordinarily push their college, a counselor who sees you as a strong candidate may try to impress you with the college's numerous merits to convince you to apply.

Chapter 9

Other Types of Interviews

The Student Interview

In addition to the interview with an admissions counselor, some colleges will want you to have an on-campus personal interview with a student, and what you get is the luck of the draw. Students don't usually sit in on the admissions discussions, but their interview notes are filed in your application folder. You may find it easier to talk with a student, but your objectives should remain the same no matter who does the interviewing. (See Chapter 10, *Putting Your Best Foot Forward.*)

The Alumni Interview

Still another kind of personal interview is with an alumnus or alumna of the college who lives in your area. You should take advantage of the alumni interview whenever it is offered, even if you've had an on-campus interview. The more people you talk to about the college, the better off you are. You will know more about the college and more people will know about you.

The alumni interview is usually arranged by the college after you have applied, and is typically held in the interviewer's home or office, often lasting an hour or more. Alumni are customarily selected by the college and briefed on interview procedures. The interviewer may be an older, more traditional graduate or a recent graduate closer in age to you. Many colleges value the input of the alumni interviewer, who is one more person who has seen you "up close," so don't treat the interview any differently than you would an on-campus one.

Group Interviews

Another type of interview is the on-campus informational group interview. More and more colleges are turning to this type of session, finding it a better use of their staff's time.

Parents and students are invited to meet with an admissions staff member in small groups. The counselor talks about the college, sometimes illustrating his or her account with a video presentation, and then asks for questions from the group. This is a good time for you to ask questions, and you can learn from listening to others' queries about things that may not have occurred to you. Because this type of interview is for information only, and is nonevaluative and nonjudgmental, you may find it less intimidating.

Group sessions are also utilized when the college representative, most often an admissions counselor who covers your geographical area, visits your locality or your high school. Take advantage of this opportunity to hear about the college and ask questions. After the session, introduce yourself to the representative and mention that you are planning to visit, or that you already have. Show interest, but don't monopolize the person and prevent other students from talking.

The Audition

Music conservatories, drama schools, and dance departments hold auditions rather than interviews to evaluate candidates. The audition is held on specific dates at the college or in centrally located cities around the country. It is best to know well in advance when you will audition and what is expected. The music school will ask you to perform several types of music representing different styles and periods, the drama school to present several memorized selections, and the dance department to demonstrate your technique in a dance class. You should rehearse your pieces with your teacher or group well before staging the real thing.

Art schools have their own version of an audition—the portfolio. Each art school has special requirements, so check with each place well ahead of time to make sure you have appropriate material.

Auditions and portfolios are different from interviews in that they are usually required and play an important role in the admissions decision.

Special-Interest Interviews

If you are an athlete and want to play on a college team, talk to the coach in your sport. Arrange this ahead of time with the admissions secretary or the athletic department, and bring along your scrapbook, statistics, or other pertinent information that will help the coach learn about your talents. Your high school coach may want to send a letter in advance, or you may bring it with you. In any case, you can ask the college coach about your chances of making the team. You should also try to watch the team practice or play a game to get an idea of its caliber and spirit.

If you are interested in a particular field of study and want to find out more about it, speak to students who are majoring in that subject and make an appointment with a faculty member in the department. There is no better way to find out about the specifics of a department than to talk with the people directly involved.

If you are interested in any extracurricular activity, such as the newspaper, orchestra, radio station, intramural sports, or cheerleading, try to speak to participating students. You'll find out what the activities are like and what your chances are of getting involved.

You can use the checklist on the next page to keep track of your college interviews. Make enough photocopies of the blank checklist to cover all your interviews.

Checklist for Interviews

College Name _____

    Personal Interview   Date _____   Time _____

    Interviewer _____

    Acknowledgment Note _____

    Alumni Interview   Date _____   Time _____

    Interviewer _____

    Acknowledgment Note _____

    Group Interview   Date _____   Time _____

    College Representative _____

    Athletic Interview   Date _____   Time _____

    Coach _____

    Audition   Place _____   Date _____   Time _____

    Requirements _____

Comments:

Chapter 10

Putting Your Best Foot Forward

Your Mental Approach

Interviewing skill is not something you are born with, but it is something you can learn. For starters, put aside the notion that the interview is an interrogation where you'll be bombarded with questions. Think of it as an exchange between two people learning about each other. And don't think the interviewer is looking for a certain type—he or she wants to talk to a *real* person, YOU. You don't have to pose, fake it, or be someone you're not. BE YOURSELF. The golden rule for interviews is: *Know thyself and to thine own self be true.* That's what it's all about.

Know Thyself

You are visiting colleges and having interviews *before* you apply, so the interviewer doesn't have a folder on you, and therefore knows nothing about you until you speak up. Sometimes you may be asked to fill out a brief questionnaire with your name, high school, and course schedule, but generally the counselor doesn't know anything about you when you walk into the room. Your assignment in putting your best foot forward is to familiarize the interviewer with your distinctive personality. To do that, *you must know yourself.*

One reason for interview anxiety is that you may not be accustomed to thinking about yourself in an organized, lucid manner. If you're asked a personal question that you haven't thought about before, you might be surprised and thrown off base. The better you understand yourself beforehand, the more likely it is that you'll be confident dealing with anything that comes up. Effort spent getting to know yourself on your own time will pay big dividends. You won't be caught unawares if you do your soul-searching *before* the first interview. Here's how to begin.

☐ Analyze your personality

☐ Consider your strengths and weaknesses

☐ Assess your academic experience

☐ Evaluate your outside interests and activities

☐ Examine your values and goals

☐ Clarify what's important to you

Soul-searching requires time and patience. We all have impressions about ourselves, but we seldom take the time to organize what we know into a "self-portrait." Keep in mind that you must be fair to yourself in your exploration. Don't underrate or exaggerate, and don't be so hard on yourself that your portrait is unrecognizable to those who know you well. Get feedback from your parents, friends, and teachers to gauge if you're on the right track.

There are a number of ways to figure out your personal traits and qualities. Start with some words you might use to describe yourself. The "Know Thyself Vocabulary" provides an array of adjectives patterned after a list in the *Georgetown University Law Center Career Handbook*. Check off all the words that apply to you, add ones that aren't included, and explore the pattern that emerges.

Know Thyself Vocabulary

____reliable	____outgoing	____thoughtful
____sociable	____eager	____considerate
____enthusiastic	____determined	____trustworthy
____bookish	____cooperative	____independent
____relaxed	____curious	____generous
____understanding	____lively	____good natured
____calm	____idealistic	____entrepreneurial
____hardworking	____motivated	____frank
____confident	____supportive	____organized
____friendly	____sincere	____sensible
____fun loving	____conscientious	____consistent
____analytical	____persevering	____inventive
____loyal	____stable	____intellectual
____spontaneous	____alert	____tactful
____original	____assertive	____mature
____modest	____broadminded	____successful
____practical	____serious	____capable
____tenacious	____thorough	____clever
____helpful	____logical	____quick
____strong minded	____imaginative	____honest
____cheerful	____forceful	____polite
____ambitious	____rational	____poised
____reflective	____fair minded	____empathetic
____daring	____realistic	____conservative
____articulate	____private	____warm

Know Thyself Vocabulary (Continued)

____optimistic   ____liberal   ____individualistic

____resourceful   ____introspective   ____academic

____supportive   ____courageous   ____energetic

____progressive   ____deliberate   ____flexible

____bold   ____quiet   ____funny

____sensitive   ____formal   ____persuasive

____creative   ____easygoing   ____responsible

____patient   ____active   ____purposeful

____adaptable   ____sharp   ____competitive

____adventurous   ____versatile   ____firm

____strong   ____happy   ____clearheaded

____careful   ____tolerant   ____agreeable

____natural   ____attentive   ____industrious

_____other

Your Academic Self

Another facet to consider for determining the real you is your academic background and interests. Be able to describe your high school to someone who isn't familiar with it. Is the student body diverse or homogeneous? Do students and teachers respect learning and academic success? What is the quality of the teaching? Have any teachers inspired you and added to your school experience? Have they helped you develop your talents and interests? Do you think your school has prepared you for college study, or are there areas in which you feel weak? Do you think your school has limited you in any way? How competitive is the atmosphere?

Consider the subjects you've enjoyed. Are there any areas of special interest to you? Have you written any papers or been involved in any important projects? Have any of these led to further interests in or out of school? Connie, for example, became interested in prison reform because of a paper she wrote on women in prison; Doug began writing poetry after reading Walt Whitman. Frank's project on Martin Luther King, Jr., stimulated his interest in black history. Perhaps a paper you wrote had a similar effect on you.

Reflect on your academic program. What are your strongest subjects? Have you explored any subject in depth? Has there been a course that was difficult for you? How did you handle it? Were there any special factors that made it difficult? Perhaps there have been external circumstances that interfered with your academic performance like parents' divorce, dyslexia, or frequent family moves. (See "Dealing with Special Problems and Circumstances" in this chapter.)

Determine if your marks are a true estimate of your ability and potential. How do you feel about school work? Are you taking honors classes, or are you happier enrolled in regular courses? Have you done just enough to get by? Have you ever been challenged to work harder than you thought possible? Would you say you are an above average, average, or below average student? By defining your performance, purpose, and interest in school, you'll get a good idea of your academic self.

The Nonacademic You

Another dimension of your personality is revealed through the activities you've been engaged in after school and during the summer. Where have you put most of your energies and talents? What activities have meant the most to you? Have you contributed to your school or your community? How have you spent your summer vacations? Have you attained any leadership position, or won any awards? Do your activities demonstrate your competence, talent, or commitment?

For example, Liz was involved with the school and county bands and Steve taught himself the guitar. Mike was in any organization that had soccer in its name, and Rob was completing an Eagle Scout merit badge. Connie spent two afternoons a week at a soup kitchen, and Julia was a sprinter on the track team. Roger marched in the drum and bugle corps;

Checklist of Activities

- ☐ Academic honor society
- ☐ Art
  - ☐ ceramics
  - ☐ fashion
  - ☐ film
  - ☐ photography
  - ☐ studio
  - ☐ other
- ☐ Athletics_____(sport)
  - ☐ intramural
  - ☐ community
  - ☐ recreation
  - ☐ j.v.
  - ☐ varsity
- ☐ Civic affairs
- ☐ Community service
- ☐ Dance
- ☐ Debating or forensics
- ☐ Drama or theater
- ☐ Ethnic or cross-cultural activity
- ☐ Foreign exchange or study abroad
- ☐ Foreign-language activity
- ☐ Journalism
- ☐ Literary activity

- ☐ Math or computer activity
- ☐ Music
  - ☐ instrumental
  - ☐ vocal
- ☐ Outdoor interests
- ☐ Political activity
- ☐ Religious activity
- ☐ Science activity
- ☐ School-spirit activity
- ☐ Student government
- ☐ T.V. or radio
- ☐ Volunteer work
- ☐ Work
- ☐ Clubs

_____
_____

- ☐ Other activities

_____
_____
_____

- ☐ Other interests

_____
_____
_____
_____
_____

Winona marched for Native American rights. Jeff perfected his tennis game, Doug his poetry; Kunio worked for a pizza place, Lucy for SADD (Students Against Drunk Drivers). Jim led the student government; Scott delivered newspapers. While Mandy endured the rigors of Outward Bound, Keith biked all over the countryside. Any activities like these that you've engaged in are an important part of your nonacademic self.

Use the "Checklist of Activities" to indicate the activities in which you've been involved. This list is similar to the Student Descriptive Questionnaire in the *Registration Bulletin* for the SAT and may be familiar to you.

Other Considerations

To talk about yourself in a meaningful way and project the real you, be aware of the goals and values that reflect your personality. Mandy cherished closeness with her friends, Rob steered his life according to the Boy Scouts' tenets, and Liz expressed herself through her music. Connie's life was enriched by helping others; Karen's religion gave her strength; Rachel believed honesty counted most; and José expected to serve his community. Do you have a star you steer by? What is it you care about?

Think about what you want to accomplish in the years ahead and how you would like to grow. Have there been any significant persons, events, or experiences that have shaped your development or your way of thinking? Be ready to talk about such meaningful experiences in your life.

Sometimes it is easier to think about yourself with a list of questions in mind. Some of the following have been used by interviewers to learn more about applicants. Mull them over to get a clear idea of who you are, what makes you tick, what you've been doing, and where you're headed.

Twenty Questions

- ☐ What three adjectives would your best friend use to describe you?
- ☐ What have you enjoyed most about your high school years?
- ☐ How have you grown or changed?
- ☐ What activities have you found most satisfying?
- ☐ What things do you do well? What are your talents?
- ☐ What strengths would you most like to develop?
- ☐ Have any of your courses challenged you? Which ones? How?
- ☐ Are you satisfied with your accomplishments so far?
- ☐ How do you respond to academic pressure or competition?
- ☐ What would you change about your school if you had the chance?
- ☐ What do you do for relaxation? For fun?
- ☐ How do you define success?
- ☐ What do you want from life?
- ☐ How would you describe your family? Your community?

- [ ] What issues concern you?
- [ ] Are there any books or articles that have had an impact on you?
- [ ] Is there an author, activity, or field you've explored in depth?
- [ ] Have you had any stimulating intellectual experiences recently?
- [ ] How do you spend your summers?
- [ ] If you had a year to do anything you wanted, what would you do?

Letting the Real You Shine Through

Now that you have started thinking about yourself, determine which aspects are important. Ask yourself what specific points you want the interviewer to know. What important matters do you want to impart to the interviewer *before* you leave the office? Make a list of several ideas that you want to discuss, and develop a *concept* of yourself that you want to get across.

Think through how you would project this special blend of qualities to the interviewer. You don't want to puff yourself up by boasting about your assets, and you don't want to hide the real you by mumbling or whispering. You don't have to be a comedian, a hotshot, or a study in seriousness, and you don't want to be arrogant or self-important. You do want to be *honest, up front*, and *positive*. You want to express your good qualities, activities, and interests, highlighting your involvement and your personality. *Figure out how to be your own advocate.*

It is a good idea to talk about any strong interest developed over time, but it's not enough just to say you've been involved. You have to be able to discuss that activity's meaning for you. If you've been a ballet dancer since age seven, reflect on why you've stuck with it despite its hardships. If your main interest has been running track, be prepared to talk about your reasons for participating in it and the satisfactions you've had. If you've been in every show your school's put on, discuss the importance of those shows in your life. If you've worked in the student store, be able to say what it taught you about yourself and working with others. If you've been practicing to be a

Superbowl announcer, or to be first violin in a symphony orchestra, account for your interest and experience.

Whether you've been a joiner or a loner, a musician or a bookworm, a tinkerer or a scientist, a leader or a follower, a cheerleader or a biker, plan to talk about yourself with insight and discernment. Demonstrate that you've thought about yourself. Express your own point of view and your own spirit.

Treat the interview as an opportunity to discuss the importance of your activities, what gives them meaning. In the January 1986 issue of *Glamour* magazine, an admissions dean said that "Your goal is to show yourself at your strongest. If you talk about things that really matter to you, not what you think *ought* to matter, then you'll have a good interview." Mike realized that his soccer experiences had given him insights into his competitiveness; Lucy became a SADD activist to cope with the death of a classmate; Marge's cheerleading awakened her to the value of cooperation and teamwork. They all told their interviewer about these experiences as a way of communicating what mattered to them, and you should do the same.

Dealing with Special Problems and Circumstances

Most students have experienced the pressure of juggling academics, athletics, and social life, and have had some rough moments in the process. There are also students who have gone through a special experience or lived with unusual challenges that have had a significant effect on their high school experience.

John, who had always been the butt of fat-boy jokes in junior high, found new social status when he lost pounds and gained friends. In high school he was suddenly so besieged with social dates that his schoolwork took a back seat. His grades plummeted as his social life soared. Realizing at the end of junior year that he was headed for the point of no return, John took a new tack and began to get things together. He managed, by dint of really concerted effort, to bring his grades up to a more respectable level. His early academic record, however, was a disaster. His college adviser suggested that in the interview he meet the problem head on by dealing openly with the reasons for his past record and demonstrating that his present grades were a better indication of his ability.

Nora didn't consider her visual impairment a handicap to learning. She kept up with her classmates, played the flute, participated in student government, and had good friends. In the interview, she discussed her disability as a personal characteristic, but didn't dwell on it. She focused instead on the abilities which were evident in her record, activities, and goals.

All through high school Sarah had actively expressed her liberal point of view. In her junior year she ran into a conservative history teacher who didn't respect opinions that differed markedly from his own. He seemed to take an instant dislike to Sarah's outspokenness, rarely called on her, and sometimes ridiculed her in front of her classmates. He was very critical of all her papers and consistently gave her low marks. It was an intolerable situation that began to affect Sarah's work not only in history, but in her other classes as well. The term ended with a marked deterioration in Sarah's grades. In her senior year, Sarah passed with flying colors, but she still had this one bad semester on her transcript, and she thought the history teacher might even have written a negative report for the record. Assuming that she shouldn't complain about a teacher to the admissions people, Sarah didn't know how to deal with the problem. After discussing the dilemma with her parents and her school counselor, Sarah decided to lay her cards on the interview table. Her approach was not to whine or gripe, but to explain forthrightly how her liberal viewpoint had clashed with her teacher's conservative ideas, and the overall effect this experience had had on her schoolwork. After giving the subject much thought, Sarah was ready to discuss what she had learned about coping with a stressful situation.

All during junior high, the tension between Scott's parents had increased until they finally sought a divorce, with Scott a pawn in their battle. Scott was emotionally torn apart. Everything around him seemed to be disintegrating. He struggled to maintain his equilibrium, but he had a hard time keeping his mind on his school work. Eventually, with the help of his close friends and their parents, he got his act together and began salvaging his academic and social life. Having learned a lot about himself, Scott chose to talk about these special circumstances in his interview, providing the admissions counselor with a fuller understanding of his background.

Kim's father was a Navy man who was periodically transferred to different posts. Every time they moved, Kim had to cope with a new neighborhood, new friends, and new school. Although none of this came easily, Kim found excitement and adventure in each relocation. She thought that her college interviewer would be interested in her experiences.

Admissions counselors *are* interested in hearing about any special situations that affected you. They want to know how you've handled difficult experiences and about any extra effort you've had to make because of extenuating circumstances.

Not all difficult situations or problem areas are subjects for a college interview, however. Talk over your individual case with a teacher, your parents, or an adult close to you to decide whether discussing your particular situation is appropriate.

Practice Interviews

To give you an extra dose of confidence before you venture out for the real thing, you may decide to have a practice interview. Invite a friend to role-play with you, each of you taking turns as the interviewer and the interviewee. Ask a neighbor or a friend of the family to conduct a mock interview. Or perhaps you know someone who does job interviewing who will rehearse with you. You might enjoy taping the session, although hearing and/or seeing yourself on tape for the first time is usually a shock. It may, however, give you an insight into how you project yourself.

Use the questions in this chapter and in chapters 13 and 14, *Questions Interviewers Ask, Questions to Ask Your Interviewer*, as starting points for your practice. *Don't*, however, *memorize a speech* and don't prepare so carefully that you sound like a preprogrammed robot. You want to *preserve your spontaneity* and your ability to respond to the individuality of the interviewer. Remember, you're preparing a concept, not a script.

One practice strategy that gives you a taste of the real thing is to start your interviews at a college where your admission chances are pretty good. Save the interviews at your "reach" colleges for later in the season when you have gained some experience. (See "Best Timing" in Chapter 11.)

Putting your best foot forward means projecting yourself in a pleasant, polite, *thought-through* manner that will make

Checklist for Putting Your Best Foot Forward

Know Thyself

 Know your academic self
 Know the nonacademic you
 Know your goals and values
 Answer the Twenty Questions

Shine Through

 Be yourself
 Be positive
 Be honest
 Be ready
 Be polite

Don'ts

 Don't pose
 Don't whisper
 Don't be arrogant
 Don't memorize

you a long-remembered candidate. The better you understand yourself, the more likely you'll *be yourself* in the interview. When a question comes around requiring you to talk about yourself, you'll be ready.

Chapter 11

Planning for the Interview

What to Wear

A few days before the first interview, Andy's father considered buying him some Brooks Brothers clothes so he wouldn't appear at the college in torn jeans and dirty Nikes, but Andy refused to go wearing preppy attire. Marge, however, thought she ought to get all dressed up for her visit to the campus, but she wasn't quite sure what that meant. Grace wanted to stand out from the crowd and contemplated wearing her punky all-black outfit.

Although dress isn't crucial, it does count. The interviewer's first impression is based on how you look. If Shakespeare was right in thinking "apparel oft proclaims the man," then Andy's torn jeans bespoke a careless attitude that was misleading. As much as Andy resented getting cleaned up, and as much as he professed a "take-me-as-I-am" attitude, he had to confess that he wasn't indifferent to the interview.

The importance of clothes is in helping you *make a good first impression*. Just as you wouldn't wear torn jeans or flashy clothes to a job interview, you shouldn't wear them to a college interview. Feel comfortable and at ease in what you wear, but since you aren't going to a picnic or a ballgame, leave your favorite T-shirt and rubber hunting shoes at home. *Neat and clean* are the rules for this trip. Dress for a business meeting, not a dance or a party, and wear clothes suitable for a moderately formal occasion. At the same time, don't wear an outfit right off the rack, as you're probably more comfortable with something tried and true. If you haven't donned a tie and jacket before, this isn't the time to do so.

Your aim is to *look and feel your best*. If, like Grace, you must make a statement with your clothes, you better be prepared to gab about your garb, as it won't go unnoticed. Your costume might provide just the opening for an interesting conversation about your views on conformity. According to one admissions counselor, attitude is quite important: "We won't hold a mohawk or a punk style against a student, but we sure would like to know if it's mere self-indulgence." On the other hand, you don't have to "dress for success" in a nondescript uniform. As an eastern seaboard counselor put it, "You definitely don't have to wear a shirtwaist dress or a silk tie, but please don't come dressed for a beach party, wearing sunglasses and chewing gum."

In general, pressed trousers, a clean, quiet dress shirt (with or without a tie), or a trim turtleneck, and a sweater or a jacket are appropriate for men. Shoes are better than sneakers, and all laces should be tied. One admissions counselor from a mid-Atlantic college warns: "Sloppy doesn't cut the mustard here. Nobody minds jeans and a sweater as long as they're neat and clean, but for heaven's sake, tie the laces and wear some socks."

A skirt or slacks, a neat blouse with a jacket or sweater, or a simple dress in a subdued color are suitable for women. Jewelry, such as earrings, should be tasteful, and shoes should fit the apparel, and be neither too dressy nor too informal. Try to have a put-together look. A Midwestern admissions counselor advises: "Clothes do make a difference. Artsy clothes are fine, but ripped up jeans a no-no. We don't require a uniform, but we do like to think you've put some thought into your appearance."

You may not want to call undue attention to yourself as you stroll on the campus, so it's a good idea to have casual clothes to wear before and after the interview. To get an idea of what students are currently wearing, browse through the pictures in the viewbook or catalog. This will tell you whether the clothes you have picked out are suitable, but remember that you want to be yourself and not a copy of anyone.

Mind Your P's and Q's

Having planned your outfit, there are now some other matters to attend to in preparation for the interview. These include:

The Three P's	The Two Q's
1. Be prepared	1. Don't quibble or complain
2. Be prompt	2. Ask questions
3. Be polite	

Be Prepared

One of the points that admissions counselors across the country agree on is that *students should come prepared.* Admissions people enjoy talking to students who have given the college—and the interview—some real thought. This means knowing beforehand as much about the college as possible. You'll be well informed if you study the current course catalog (see Chapter 6, *How to Read a College Catalog*) and jot down any questions you have. Doug wanted to clarify the academic requirements for a foreign language, and Jeff the opportunities for study abroad. Connie asked about the college's academic strengths, and Mandy the number of women graduates who were accepted into law school.

As you tour the campus, other issues will come up. You may be interested in how to get on the newspaper staff, how the college chooses freshman roommates, what services there are for the visually impaired, the role fraternities play, or the geographic diversity of the students. All these subjects indicate your interest in delving deeper into the character of the college. Admissions counselors always enjoy meeting students who ask discerning questions not already answered in the catalog. (See "Best Timing" in this chapter.)

Another way to prepare is to *know yourself* (see Chapter 10, *Putting Your Best Foot Forward*). Understand your strengths, special qualities, talents, values, and goals, and be aware of your weaknesses. Be ready to talk about yourself—and not like a steamroller or in a whisper, but clearly and distinctly in your natural voice. If you clam up or answer in monosyllables, the interviewer won't learn much about you. Practice talking in sentences and paragraphs, and learn to describe what is important to you. This is not the time to keep your good points under wraps.

Admissions interviewers appreciate talking to students who aren't echoes of other students. Do your homework to understand both yourself and the college, project your special qualities, and you'll be a hit.

Be Prompt

It should go without saying that you should be *on time* for your interview. Plan to reach the admissions office 5 or 10 minutes before the scheduled appointment. Use this interval to freshen up, think about the points you want to make, collect your thoughts, and then walk into the interview relaxed and confident. Your interview may last as long as an hour, so don't set up another appointment or arrange your ride to the airport without giving yourself plenty of time. Allow time to mull over the interview in a quiet place before you proceed to your next destination.

Be Polite

Bring your best manners with you to the interview. If the interviewer offers his or her hand, shake it firmly. Since your handshake and your clothes are the first quick impressions the counselor has, don't be limp as a dishrag or use a vise grip. Practice at home if necessary.

Wait until you're asked to sit down, and then sit up straight (not ramrod straight, just easy straight). Be relaxed, but don't slump, sprawl, or lean into the interviewer so that you are nose to nose. Show you're ready to talk by your alert, respectful attitude. Address the interviewer by name, or "sir" or "ma'am" if that is comfortable for you. Don't smoke, don't chew gum, don't swear.

Interviewers are skilled at putting you at ease, but each has a different style and personality. If the interviewer's approach is to tell jokes, smile or laugh if you wish, but don't think you have to. Above all, don't try to compete in the joke category. You may not hit it off with all the interviewers you meet, so don't panic if things aren't going as well as you'd hoped. Sometimes it's the interviewer who's having a bad day, not you.

The interviewer will signal that the end of the session is near by making a wrap-up statement, pulling papers together, getting up and motioning for you to do the same, or saying something to that effect. Don't begin talking suddenly about a new subject or try to continue the conversation. If you have more questions, ask the counselor if you might pose them in a letter. Create the right impression with a *pleasant, straightforward manner, a firm handshake, and a polite thank you.*

When you get home, don't hesitate to write a note to your interviewer, asking those unanswered questions, clarifying a point, or commenting on your visit. One admissions counselor considers notes a confirmation of good manners; another appreciates them so much he keeps them in a "We Love You" file.

Don't Quibble or Complain

Don't pick a fight with the interviewer. Don't walk into the interview with a chip on your shoulder. This isn't the moment to correct the counselor's grammar or quibble about the pronunciation of a word. If there is a controversy, stand up for your point of view, but be tactful and courteous.

Don't complain about all the wrongs done to you. Don't be like Albert, who blamed his math teachers for his bad marks, or Stella, who thought her chemistry teacher had it in for her. Both were ready to accuse their teachers and excuse themselves—don't you do the same. If there is a special circumstance that needs explaining, present it in a straightforward manner so that both you and the teacher share the involvement. A good motto to bring with you is: *Accentuate the positive; eliminate the negative.*

Take responsibility for the grades you received unless there are extraordinary extenuating circumstances. Occasionally you may get into a situation where you and a teacher have just not seen eye to eye. Analyze the situation beforehand and see if you can come up with a forthright way to deal with it, as Sarah did. (See Chapter 10, *Putting Your Best Foot Forward*.)

Ask Questions

One of your principal objectives in the interview is to find out more about the college. Don't be afraid to ask anything and everything you want to know—making sure, of course, that your queries aren't already answered in the literature the college has sent you. There's no sense in asking if there's an anthropology department when you can look it up in the catalog.

But don't ask questions just for asking's sake or pose as an expert in something you know little about. Interviewers are plenty savvy. Having spoken with hundreds of students, they can spot show-off and off-the-wall questions asked merely for effect.

Admissions counselors agree that probing questions that challenge them to think, often point out a candidate's specialness. As a college shopper you must be curious. Explore your concerns, and then without hesitation or the shakes, ask questions that are relevant. You undoubtedly have found ideas in Part I, and you may get other thoughts when you read Chapter 14, *Questions to Ask Your Interviewer.*

It's okay to have a list of questions with you and refer to them as the conversation proceeds. Otherwise, know in advance what your queries are and review them in your head before the interview. Be inquiring. You are making a very expensive, important investment that you want to be sure will benefit you. You wouldn't invest in a bike or a stereo without asking the dealer lots of questions. Handle the college interview just as inquisitively.

Best Timing

When making plans for your interviews, remember "safeties first." Gain experience at your "safe" schools where the interview won't make a crucial difference and you can be more relaxed.

Schedule interviews at your most desired colleges for the end of the line when you'll be "interview seasoned," and remember to book your appointments well ahead of time because interview schedules fill up early.

Checklist of What to Do and Not Do

Do

Be neat, clean, and comfortable
Look and feel your best
Be prepared, prompt, and polite
Ask informed questions
Accentuate the positive
Be yourself
Write an acknowledgment note

Don't

Smoke, swear, or chew gum
Quibble or complain
Pose
Be passive
Whisper
Be arrogant

Try to arrange your interview toward the end of your campus visit to give yourself ample chance to look around and talk to students. Your impressions and questions will be fresh and you will have a number of things to discuss with the interviewer. (See "An Ideal Campus Schedule" in Chapter 3.)

Special Hints

☐ Don't become weary, complacent, or bored because of a heavy interview schedule. If you think you're losing your zest, take a break and regroup. Few things are as much of a turn-off to interviewers as a bored student or a know-it-all. When you arrive at your first-choice college, you should be confident *and* in good spirits.

☐ Don't bring your super term paper, poetry selections, or other long pieces of writing with you. You want the interview to be a conversation, not a reading session. Send all your special extras with your application.

☐ Don't hand over your transcript to the interviewer unless it is asked for or you have a special reason to discuss it.

After the Interview Is Over

It's always a good idea to sit down in a quiet place and review how the interview went. If you missed some good openings or didn't get across some important points, you can follow up with a letter. Think about ways you can avoid letting that happen in future interviews. Don't worry if you think the interview didn't go just right; not all interviews will be four-star experiences, and you are probably your own worst critic. Remember, also, that the interview isn't the only, or the most important, part of your application. Do your part by preparing for the interview and feeling comfortable being yourself and things will go well.

Chapter 12

Tips for the Shy Person

The Problem

Ever since he could remember, George tried to disappear into his surroundings and avoid being "put on the spot." He never raised his hand in class; he blushed when he was called upon to speak; he couldn't tell a joke or laugh at himself; and his stomach went into knots at parties. He was especially unsure of himself in new situations.

With college time approaching, and with it the necessity of talking to complete strangers on campus visits and in interviews, George almost panicked. His normal fear of new situations was intensified by the frightening prospect of revealing himself to people he didn't know. George assumed he would be a failure, stammering and blushing during the interview, and walking around each new campus without talking to a soul. All his life he had tried to hide his shyness, but he knew that for his college search he would be compelled to deal with it or face the prospect of not applying to colleges where visits and interviews were important. That would limit his chances of making the right college choice.

George's concerns are typical of a shy person, but he is not alone. Almost everyone has experienced some degree of shyness in new situations. Some people hang back in social encounters, feeling ill at ease in a room full of strangers, waiting for someone else to take the lead. Others may experience a mild physical reaction such as damp palms, a dry mouth, or a rapid heart beat. In *The Shy Person's Book*, Claire Rayner says that those with a greater degree of shyness display reactions that range from a parched throat to a voice so low that it cannot be heard; from squeaking to stammering; from mild to severe perspiring; from going pale to blushing; from a thick lumping in the throat to a relentless thumping in the chest to a bobbing head caused by severe neck tremors. Some talk so much at a high speed that they cannot be interrupted; others adopt a blustery, hale and hearty manner to try to hide inner nervousness.

George's reactions were on the extreme end of the scale. In everyday new situations he had so much trouble keeping his physical symptoms under control that he sometimes didn't even hear what people said to him. In the interview, he feared he wouldn't know what to say if he were asked a direct question, or worse, he would make a fool of himself by saying something silly. He dreaded not only the interviews, but the campus visit as well. The mere notion of wandering about a strange place and staying overnight with someone he didn't know made him panicky. Although George didn't want to surrender his option of having good college choices, he didn't know how to cope with his problem. He tried to forget it, but it wouldn't go away. George finally decided to talk to his parents about his painful predicament. After quietly listening to his disturbing account, his parents helped George organize a plan.

Acknowledging the Problem

Discussing his problem with his parents was a good decision. The first step toward overcoming a shyness problem is to acknowledge it. The second step is to want to change. Once faced, there are ways to deal with it. Shy people differ not so much in the degree of shyness they suffer from, but in how each copes with his or her problem.

If you think you share elements of George's uneasiness in facing the campus visit and the interview, here are some ways to prepare yourself.

Practice Talking

If you are fortunate enough to have someone, a friend or a relative, with whom you can share this difficulty, set up some situations where you *talk about yourself* on a steady basis. It is important that you practice talking aloud about yourself, for that's what you'll be doing in the interview. Speak about a project you're working on, a paper you're writing, or a problem in school. Begin with information about the topic and move into how *you* feel about it, how it is relevant to you. Put yourself into the information. What do you like about the project? What did you learn from the subject? State something about the topic that interests you. Practice speaking in the first person singular. Use the words, "I think," "I feel," or "This is the way it strikes me." Don't be afraid that you'll be boring. And remember that it will take time to feel comfortable communicating with another person, especially if you've been avoiding such situations.

To help George become accustomed to talking about himself, his parents launched "take a topic to dinner." Every night they encouraged George to talk about a school event. At first he was halting and uncomfortable, but gradually he began to unwind. When he became more at ease, they suggested more complex topics such as hopes for the future or goals that each member of the family wanted to achieve. George's two older brothers, who usually monopolized the mealtime conversation, began listening to George and talking with him instead of at him. Pretty soon the family began having shared dinner conversations with George as a participant rather than a full-time silent listener. Still later, his parents suggested that each person tell a joke, and they helped George overcome his awkwardness by having him read the joke aloud first. Getting this kind of practice helped George acquire self-confidence, which loosened his tensions about talking about himself.

Strategies for Those with No One to Turn to

George was lucky that he had family support in his efforts to handle his shyness, but not everyone is that fortunate. If you don't have someone with whom you can talk, there are other approaches you can take, but remember, they take time, patience, and practice.

One measure is to write down your statement about a project, paper, or school problem and then read it aloud in front of a mirror or an empty chair. Put the paper away and speak your piece. Try this several times a week. Write about a different topic and follow the same procedure the next week. Don't forget to put yourself into the statement. Use the first person singular. Even though you may feel silly doing this, it will give you practice talking out loud about yourself.

If you have a tape recorder, you might want to record your statement. Talking into a recorder simulates, in a small way, the experience of talking to an audience. It also helps to hear how you sound, but don't be shocked on hearing your voice for the first time. Most people don't like their own voice at first.

After you have read your written statements about a school issue several times, practice talking about a personal experience. Speak aloud about something that happened to you at school. Talk to the mirror or chair. If something funny happened, don't be afraid to verbalize it. Do this activity several times.

Next, state a belief that is important to you. Speak in the first person. Express out loud the feelings and experiences that led you to this belief. Personal beliefs might include the importance of your family, or what you think about honesty, or the value of friendship, or religion. Whatever your beliefs, articulating them will help you better present what you've learned about who you are and what makes you tick. Continue these activities every day. Don't give up.

Another technique is to keep a journal detailing the events of the day. Read the entry aloud in front of a mirror. Get accustomed to hearing your voice say "I." Practice, practice, practice talking aloud.

These exercises will boost your ability to talk about yourself and give you the confidence to present yourself at your strongest in the interview.

Other Tips

To enable you to become more comfortable talking to strangers, Philip Zimbardo, in his book *Shyness*, recommends practicing talking on the phone. He suggests calling a department store and checking on the price of an advertised item, calling a movie house and asking for show times, or calling the library and asking the reference librarian what the population of the United States is or any other information you'd like to know.

Books on shyness also recommend talking to strangers in safe, public places. One tactic is to speak to a salesperson in a store. Ask about how an item works or what other colors it comes in, and spend at least 30 seconds talking. Another approach is to go to the library and ask a librarian where the college directories are and tell her why you are looking. Don't be afraid to say, "I'm a senior in high school beginning my college search, and I need some help."

Still another recommended exercise in safely talking to a stranger can take place when you're in the check-out line of a store, by striking up a conversation about a common experience you are sharing. Talk to the clerk or the person behind you about the weather, or the crowds, or the lack of crowds. An opening remark might be a positive statement such as, "It's such a nice day! It makes me want to be out hiking in the country." Or, "I like shopping in this store. The salespeople are so pleasant." Other places where you can practice overcoming shyness are movie lines, the school cafeteria, or sports events.

The Bowers, authors of *Asserting Yourself*, suggest writing down facts about each of these "greeting-talk" conversations: 1) where it took place, 2) with whom, 3) what you said, 4) what the other person said, 5) what your reactions were, 6) how you felt about yourself. This will help you clue into what really happens in public socializing.

Another way to learn to express yourself vocally is to go up after class and ask a teacher about an assignment, or about a theme you wrote, or about anything else that is relevant. Practice out loud what you'll say beforehand, but don't memorize a script. If you feel more confident writing it down in advance, just scribble a few key words, not whole sentences.

If there is a particular teacher who you think may be sympathetic, try enlisting his or her help. Explain your problem and what you're doing to overcome it. Perhaps the teacher will have helpful suggestions.

Other places where talking is a necessity are drama clubs, speech classes, and forensics societies. If your school or community has one of these groups, investigate and see if you want to join. You may first have to overcome some of your apprehensions, but it might prove to be just the ticket.

People who deal with shyness recommend learning a joke, writing it down, and then practicing telling it to yourself out loud. After you have mastered it, tell it to a friend or a small group of people.

Remember that the objective of these exercises is getting accustomed to talking out loud and communicating with others. It won't happen overnight, and you have to practice.

Listed below are several books that suggest useful ways to deal with shyness; your library may have others.

Sharon Anthony Bower and Gordon H. Bower. *Asserting Yourself*. Reading, Mass.: Addison-Wesley, 1976.

Gerald M. Phillips. *Help for Shy People*. Englewood Cliffs, N.J.: Prentice-Hall, 1981.

Claire Rayner. *The Shy Person's Book*. London: Wolfe, 1973.

Arthur C. Wassmer. *Making Contact*. New York: Dial Press, 1978.

Philip G. Zimbardo. *Shyness*. Reading, Mass.: Addison-Wesley, 1981.

Dealing with Questions

Once you feel somewhat more at ease talking about yourself to other people, you can begin to tackle the give and take of the interview process. Explore the questions in chapters 10 and 13, paying particular attention to those that are more personal in nature. Get a handle on the areas you find difficult to talk about; then concentrate on thinking these through. Write down your answers to these questions so that they make sense. Say them aloud in front of a mirror and practice looking yourself in the eye.

To get the feel of an interview from both sides of the desk, have a friend or relative do a mock interview with you and take turns playing the parts of interviewer and interviewee. The experts on shyness find that role-playing helps one acclimate to new situations. Use the questions you have worked on and continue with new ones. Don't memorize your answers, but work up to extemporizing. If this part comes too hard, go back to square one and talk about an activity important to you.

Other Steps to Take

Shy persons sometimes put people off physically by not appearing receptive. You *can* learn how to change this. One authority on shyness, Dr. Arthur C. Wassmer, recommends practicing making eye contact by concentrating on looking directly at the person with whom you're talking. Looking at a person is an indication that you *are interested* and that you are paying attention.

Another of Dr. Wassmer's recommendations is to practice smiling and nodding your head in response, indicating your interest. He also suggests sitting in a relaxed posture with hands in your lap or on the chair arms, not folded across your chest. As you do these exercises, look at the person, smile at appropriate times, nod your head in approval of a particular statement, and sit in a relaxed posture.

Relaxation Techniques

Shy persons are not the only ones nervous about the interview. Almost every student experiences some anxiety before the interview actually begins. The first 15 seconds of an interview are usually the hardest, and the interviewer is aware that the first task is to put you at ease. Remember that the interviewer wants to talk to you and wants to help you talk about yourself.

People who deal with stress suggest that each of us learn how to relax in tense situations. One of the common ways to deal with tension is to do deep breathing as follows: Take three deep breaths, using your abdominal muscles. Count to five as you breathe in, hold briefly, then breathe out in five counts. At the end of each sequence say to yourself, "om," or, "easy does it." Try this now to see if you feel more relaxed. Practice to see if you're comfortable breathing this way.

If the deep breathing isn't comfortable for you, try sitting in a relaxed position and then concentrate on breathing naturally. Breathe in and out, in and out, saying "om" to yourself after each sequence. If your mind starts wandering, bring it back to your breathing. This exercise often has the effect of easing tension.

Keep in Mind

Remember that the college interviewer is interested in *you*. He or she wants to make contact with you and is skilled in drawing you out. You must develop a willingness and desire to respond. By exploring your interests and activities—anything from comic books to baseball to music—and learning to talk about them, you will have more confidence when the interview takes place. Systematically read the preceding chapters on the interview, taking notes, following directions, and setting goals.

If you experience severe shyness during the interview and things aren't going well, a good solution is to tell the interviewer how you feel. You will probably find the interviewer receptive to your saying something like, "I'm really uncomfortable now. I'm trying to overcome my shyness, but it's hard for me to talk right at this moment." You'll be pleasantly relieved at the way most interviewers will react. However, if the interviewer is a cold fish, nothing much is going to help. You'll have to chalk that one up to experience.

When Nothing Else Works

If you find that none of these measures works for you, you may want to consult with your physician. Your doctor may prescribe a medication that actors sometimes use to block the symptoms of stage fright.

A Special Hint

More than others, the shy person needs to plan everything well in advance and follow through on the arrangements. Carefully study chapters 2, 3, and 4 for the general outline of preparations to make and things to do. If you cannot do them yourself, and many shy persons cannot, enlist your parents to assist in the preparations, making the necessary phone calls, for ex-

Checklist of Specific Preparations for the Shy Person

□ Call in advance for the interview appointment. Make sure you write down the day and time.

□ Ask where the meeting is going to take place and with whom. Become familiar with your interviewer's name.

□ Ask the admissions secretary to send you a map of the campus with the admissions office clearly marked.

□ Get directions to the campus.

□ On your first campus visit, arrange to go with your parents, a favorite relative, or a friend—whoever is supportive and makes you most comfortable.

□ For greater ease on your overnight, arrange to stay with someone you know, someone from your area, or a friend of a friend. If that's not possible, ask the admissions secretary to give you your host's phone number so that you can talk *before* your trip. The more familiar you are with your host, the easier your first meeting will be.

□ Bring a list of *written* questions. Refer to the list when talking to your host and other students.

□ If any of these steps is too difficult, ask your family to help.

ample. Don't be ashamed to ask your family for help. Remember that the goal is to enable the college to know the real you despite your shyness.

Chapter 13

Questions Interviewers Ask

"What will they ask? What kinds of questions will they stick to me? How will I know what to say?" These are the worrisome fears that most students have about the interview. By the time you reach this chapter, you should have a good notion of what the interview is all about and realize that the questions are not intended to "catch you" but rather to help you talk about yourself. Remember that one purpose of the interview is to get to know you better, and questions are a way to break the ice and get you started.

In the first few minutes of warm-up time, the admissions counselor, knowing that it is a strained situation, tries to put you at ease. He might begin with a few social amenities and pleasantries that may give you information about his role in the college or the intent and direction of the interview. If he already has some information about you, he may comment on it.

Question Categories

A standard interview then goes on to its main purpose: for the interviewer to learn more about you and for you to learn more about the college. To achieve this the interview usually covers four areas:

- ☐ Your high school experience
- ☐ The college
- ☐ You and the world around you
- ☐ Your questions

The following sections provide sample questions on these subjects that have been asked to get interviews underway. An interviewer will ask only one or two of these questions as a springboard to get things rolling. None of these questions is to be answered with a curt yes or no. The questions are meant to draw you out so that the conversation, led by a skilled admissions counselor, will flow from area to area.

Mull over these questions. Practice elaborating on your thinking. Think about the *whys* of your reactions. Formulate your responses and practice saying them out loud to your family or friends. But *don't memorize*. Your purpose in reviewing these questions is to clarify your thoughts about these subjects, not to write a script.

Questions About Your High School Experience

The questions about high school touch topics you are most familiar with: your academic background, your thoughts about high school, extracurricular activities, and your community.

Your Academic Background and School

- ☐ Tell me something about your courses.
- ☐ What courses have you enjoyed the most?
- ☐ What courses have been most difficult for you?
- ☐ What is your high school schedule?
- ☐ What satisfactions have you had from your studies?
- ☐ Has school been challenging? What course has been most challenging?

☐ What kind of student have you been? Would this change if you had the chance to do it over again?

☐ Have you worked up to your potential?

☐ Is your record an accurate gauge of your abilities and potential?

☐ Is there any outside circumstance that interfered with your academic performance?

☐ Do you like your high school?

☐ How would you describe your school?

☐ What is the range of students at your school? Where do you fit in?

☐ Do you like your teachers? What was your favorite teacher like?

☐ What has been a controversial issue in your school? What is your reaction to the controversy?

☐ If you had the chance, what changes would you make in your school?

Your Extracurricular Activities

☐ What extracurricular activity has been most satisfying to you?

☐ What is the most significant contribution you've made to your school?

☐ How would others describe your role in the school community?

☐ What activities do you enjoy most outside the daily routine of school?

☐ Do you have any hobbies or special interests?

☐ Have you worked or been a volunteer?

☐ Would you make different choices if you were to do it all over again?

☐ What do you most enjoy doing for fun? for relaxation? for stimulation?

☐ How do you spend a typical day after school?

- [ ] What do you do in your spare time?
- [ ] How did you spend last summer?
- [ ] What do you do with any money you've earned?

Your Community

- [ ] How would you describe your home town?
- [ ] Tell me something about your community.
- [ ] What has been a controversial issue in your community? What is your position on it?
- [ ] How has living in your community affected your outlook?

Questions About College

The second category of questions is about college. The basic question, one that you should give some thought to, is *why do you want to go to college*? There are variations on this theme that require further analysis, so try to think beyond the "getting a good education" response or "finding a career." Think a little harder and dig a little deeper to get answers that are true for you.

- [ ] Why do you want to go to college?
- [ ] What satisfactions do you expect to find in college?
- [ ] What are you looking forward to in college?
- [ ] What do you hope to accomplish in the next four years?
- [ ] What do you expect to get out of college?
- [ ] What do you want from an education?
- [ ] What knowledge are you seeking?
- [ ] What interests do you want to pursue in college?
- [ ] What do you hope to major in and why?
- [ ] What self-development do you see for yourself in college?
- [ ] What are some of your criteria or considerations in choosing a college?
- [ ] Why have you chosen this college to investigate?

☐ What do you want to know about us?

☐ What is of most interest to you on campus?

☐ What other colleges are you considering?

☐ What do you expect to be doing seven years from now? twelve years?

☐ Have you ever thought of not going to college? What would you do?

You and the World Around You

This third category of questions requires some soul-searching. The interviewer doesn't ask such questions to provoke you, but to dig a little deeper into your attitudes and viewpoint. This category includes what are generally appreciated as the "hard" questions, which often include some type of book question, a variation on the hero or heroine theme, more probing personal queries, and current events topics. The more selective the college, the more searching these questions tend to be. The following are sample questions, but recognize that there are as many questions as there are interviewers. However, if you can handle the following list, you'll be prepared for almost anything. Be sure you're responding with your own ideas and enthusiasms. Don't get into a hole by talking about a book you merely skimmed or a topic you're not informed about. Try out the questions, giving them some well-honed thought.

Book Questions

☐ What are you reading now that is of interest?

☐ Are there any books you've read in the last year or so that significantly affected you?

☐ What is the best book you've ever read?

☐ What three books would you take to a desert island?

☐ Are there any authors you particularly like?

☐ Any literary character you admire?

☐ What magazines do you read regularly?

☐ What TV shows do you watch?

☐ What are your favorite movies?

☐ What play, concert, museum exhibit, or dance recital have you recently attended? What is your opinion of it?

Hero or Heroine Questions

☐ Do you have any contemporary heroes?

☐ Do you have any historical heroes?

☐ What person, living or dead, would you most like to talk to and what would you talk about?

☐ What person has had the most impact on the twentieth century?

☐ What president would you most like to meet? Why?

Personal Questions

☐ What things do you do well? What are your talents?

☐ Tell me something about your family.

☐ Tell me about your upbringing. What things are important to your parents? On what issues do you have differences?

☐ What are some good decisions you've made for yourself recently?

☐ How would you describe your friendships?

☐ By whom have you been influenced?

☐ How would your best friend describe you? Would you agree?

☐ What three adjectives would you use to describe yourself?

☐ What three wishes do you have?

☐ What are your strengths? your weaknesses?

☐ What pressures do you feel to conform? How have you gone your own way?

☐ What do you think sets you apart as an individual in your school?

☐ Tell me something that has had an impact on you.

☐ What difficult situation have you been in, and how did you resolve it?

☐ What is the most difficult situation you've had to face?

☐ How would you describe your most intellectually stimulating experience?

Current Events

☐ What political or social issues should a young person be interested in?

☐ What do you think about: drug and alcohol use, gun control, nuclear freeze, nuclear power, marijuana laws, ERA, strategic defense initiative, terrorism, the latest headline?

☐ Do you ever become indignant about anything happening in the world?

☐ If you were President of the United States, what would you do about the current controversial issue?

☐ What historical event has had the most impact on the twentieth century?

☐ If you had the political power to do anything you wanted, what would you do?

Dealing with the Unexpected and Provocative

From time to time you may run across an interviewer whose style is to be provocative and to ask curve-ball questions. There isn't any way to prepare for the surprise question except to recognize that the possibility exists and that it is more likely to occur in the most selective colleges. Such interviews may be more stressful by aggressively challenging you and testing how you respond.

☐ What do you think you can do for this college?

☐ There's an invisible box on my desk with things in it that describe you. What's in the box?

☐ What would you like to talk about?

But even these questions shouldn't be threatening if you've done your homework preparing for the interview. Review the previous chapters and you'll have methods for dealing with this type of question. And bear in mind when under stress:

- ☐ Keep your responses *honest*. Don't try to fake anything.
- ☐ Keep cool. Take a deep breath and remain composed. Stressful questions reveal the interviewer's personality more than yours.
- ☐ If you don't understand the question, ask what the interviewer means.
- ☐ Don't pose as an expert on matters you know little about. It's okay to say, "I don't know."
- ☐ You can say, "I'll have to think that over. Is it okay if I write you about this?"
- ☐ Be courteous and tactful.

If you think you really haven't been given a fair shake by an intense and grilling interviewer, you may write a letter to the dean of admissions and request another interview with a different member of the admissions staff. Make sure you have correctly evaluated the situation and can back up your statement with examples.

Chapter 14

Questions to Ask
Your Interviewer

Why Ask Questions?

As a competent college shopper you facilitate your search by asking questions. You wouldn't purchase anything expensive for yourself—a stereo, bike, computer, or car—without researching it and querying the salesperson about its quality, characteristics, and shortcomings. Similarly, you must think about college as something you are buying for yourself that is more expensive and important than any of these other items. It is probably one of the more significant purchases of your shopping life. Before you pay the college bursar's fee, you want to *know as much as possible* about what you're buying. The college visit is your shopping trip and the admissions counselor is the authority on the whos, whys, and hows of the college community.

College admissions counselors genuinely enjoy talking to students. They particularly like students who have thought about the college and who want to know more about the college than is in the catalog or viewbook. They appreciate the challenge of thoughtful questions. This doesn't mean being aggressive or arrogant, nor does it mean asking smart-alecky questions, or ones for effect only. It does mean asking questions that add to your understanding of the college. The responses will help you make a good college match, so listen to them carefully. See Chapter 5, *Main Components on Campus*, for a way to organize your thoughts.

Most high school students are curious about college life, but aren't quite sure what questions to ask. The following queries will get you started. Use any or all of these questions as a springboard. Remember, the important questions are ones that interest *you*.

Question Categories

1. The students

2. Social life and campus activities

3. Campus facilities

4. The community outside the campus

5. Academics and faculty

6. Financial condition

The Students

Much of what you learn about the student body will come from personal observation and conversations with different students on campus. The admissions counselor has additional information, especially about the composition of the student body. You might begin by saying that you are interested in the makeup of students on campus and would like to know:

☐ What different kinds of people are there on campus?

☐ What region do the majority of students come from?

☐ Are there students from different types of places: cities, suburbs, small towns, rural areas? What are the percentages?

☐ From what economic bracket are the majority of students? Is there a college policy to recruit students from all brackets?

☐ What is the current percentage of students from public schools? from private schools? from parochial schools?

☐ What is the mixture of careerists, intellectuals, strivers, and loners on campus? Does any group dominate?

☐ What is the religious makeup of the student body? What religious clubs are there on campus? Do they conduct activities? How many students belong?

☐ What minorities are represented on campus? What percentage of the student body do they comprise? Are there clubs, activities, or housing that are minority related? Are there any problems? How have they been resolved?

☐ What is the percentage of foreign students, and from what countries do they hail? Are they integrated into the college community? Does the college recruit in foreign countries?

More general questions to ask might include:

☐ What do students like most about the college? like least?

☐ How important is student government in the life of the college? Has the student government made any real contribution to the school? How do you get into student government?

☐ What role do students have in shaping policy? On what committees do they sit? What voice do they have?

☐ What is the mood on campus?

☐ What were political, social, or academic issues that concerned students last year? How did the administration react? What was the resolution?

☐ How well are women accepted into the academic life of the college? Are female students' academic aspirations treated seriously? Is there any sex discrimination?

☐ Is there a drug culture on campus? How prominent is it? Is there pressure to conform?

☐ Are there any particular tensions on campus of which I should be aware?

Social Life and Campus Activities

Since students are the ones who are actively involved with the social life on campus, most of your questions in this category should be directed to them, as discussed in Chapter 5, *Main Components on Campus*. The admissions counselor may see social life in a different light, and it is valuable to get that viewpoint. The two big questions are:

☐ What do students do for fun?

☐ What happens on weekends?

You might also want to ask:

☐ What percentage of students leave campus on the weekends? (If more than 20 percent, ask why.)

☐ What is the role of fraternities and sororities on campus? If I didn't want to join, would I have a satisfactory social life? Has the administration placed any restrictions on hazing and initiation rites? How was this received?

☐ What are the dominant social groups on campus? Do the groups get along with one another? Have there been any problems?

☐ What role do team sports play in the social life of the college? What happens on football or basketball weekends? If I didn't want to join in, would I find other kindred spirits?

☐ What extracurricular activities are strongly supported by the college and the student body?

☐ How difficult is it to make a team?

☐ Are literary, artistic, and musical activities supported? How are members for these activities chosen? What voice do students have in the decisions?

☐ What activities provide a social outlet for students outside class?

☐ What were the social or cultural highlights last year?

☐ May freshmen participate in all extracurricular activities? Are there any special activities for freshmen?

☐ Are there many drinking parties on campus? Are they on weekends only, or are there parties all the time? Are there any rules or regulations governing drinking and parties?

☐ Is there an alcohol problem, and if so, how is the administration handling it?

Campus Facilities

The areas to cover in your questions are: housing; dining; activity centers and athletic and recreational facilities; health, counseling, career, and special student services, and miscellaneous; and the library.

Housing

☐ How does the college go about choosing freshman roommates?

☐ Does the college provide housing for all four years?

☐ What choices will I have as a freshman? as a sophomore? as a senior?

☐ Are the dorms quiet enough for studying? Where else do people study?

☐ Do certain types of students tend to live in particular dorms?

☐ Is there something I should know about housing here that would help me in my choice?

Dining

☐ What kinds of dining facilities exist on campus?

☐ Are there different priced meal plans? Are meal plans included in the fee structure? What is your opinion about the value of meal plans?

☐ What kinds of food plans are there: all you can eat? vegetarian? kosher?

☐ What alternative eating facilities are there on campus? Are there snack bars and coffee houses? Does the dorm have any eating facilities? May students cook in their rooms?

Activity Centers and Athletic and Recreational Facilities

☐ What kinds of facilities does the student center have? Is it a magnet for student activities? What other hangouts are there?

☐ What are the rules and regulations for recreational use of the gym facilities?

☐ What is the policy regarding women's sports?

☐ What recreational activities are there that are not described in the literature you sent me?

☐ Are practice rooms and art studios available? What arrangements would I have to make for their use?

☐ What new facilities are being planned?

☐ Is there anything special I should see before I leave?

Health, Counseling, Career, and Special Student Services, and Miscellaneous

☐ Are students satisfied with the health services offered? Are there complaints? What are they?

☐ If I have a special health problem, will I be able to handle it on campus, or will I have to go off campus?

☐ Is there a doctor, nurse, psychologist, career counselor available on campus? What is the waiting period for appointments?

☐ What statistics do you have on graduates? What percentage went on to which medical schools? law schools? business schools? graduate schools? What kinds of jobs did they get? May I have a copy of your alumni bulletin to read at home?

☐ What services are offered for special students? Is the campus completely accessible to the wheelchair bound? Are there readers for the visually impaired? Are there note-takers for the hearing impaired? Is there a counselor for disabled students?

☐ What access do freshmen have to computers or other special equipment? Are there word processors?

☐ What security measures has the college provided for students walking around late at night? Is security necessary in the dorms? Have there been any problems?

The Library

☐ Does the library have special hours during reading and exam week? Is there room for everyone who wants to study there?

☐ Are there plans for library expansion? How will that affect me during my four years?

☐ If I needed books that the library didn't have, where could I turn?

☐ What has been students' experience with the library? Have there been complaints?

☐ Has the library received any special funds recently? For what is the money being used?

The Community Outside the Campus

☐ What is there to do in town? How would I get there?

☐ How well do the college and the townspeople get along? Have they worked together on any activity? Are there tensions?

☐ Are there jobs in town for students?

Academics and Faculty

Use what you learned from your catalog reading to ask probing questions, especially about fields in which you are interested (see Chapter 6, *How to Read a College Catalog*).

☐ What is distinctive about education here?

☐ What is the educational philosophy of the college? Has it changed much in recent years?

☐ Which departments are outstanding?

☐ What areas are weak?

☐ What is the most popular major on campus? Why?

☐ What courses or professors should I be sure to take if I enroll here?

☐ How many students are in a typical freshman class? in advanced courses?

☐ Who teaches freshmen?

☐ How does freshman registration work? How easy is it to get classes I want?

☐ What are the strengths and weaknesses of your advising system?

☐ What is the quality of student and faculty relationships? Is the faculty interested in and accessible to students after class?

☐ What was the faculty turnover in the last three years? Why did faculty leave? What is the replacement policy?

☐ What percentage of faculty are part time? What departments have a high percentage of adjunct faculty?

☐ How many minority professors are there? female professors? What percentage of the faculty are they? What is the administration's policy on the hiring and promotion of minorities and women?

☐ Are curriculum changes contemplated? How will that affect my college years?

☐ Are any departments being cut back or discontinued? Why?

☐ Are any new programs scheduled for the next four years?

Financial Condition

☐ How much has the endowment grown in the last seven years?

☐ Have there been any recent fund-raising campaigns? Did the college reach its goal? What percentage of alumni contributed?

☐ Has the college recently received any special gifts? For what?

☐ Have there been any cutbacks in faculty numbers or departments in the last three years? Are any contemplated?

☐ Is a tuition hike expected?

Open Season on Questions

Now you have a good start on the kinds of questions you should be pondering. You may have more interest in a particular category, so concentrate on that area and think about what *you* want to know. It's open season on questions, so ask about anything that concerns you. Don't neglect areas that will affect your college experience. The more you know about a college, the better able you'll be to judge its qualities.

As you walk around campus and speak to students, faculty, and admissions people, you'll get the answers to many of your queries. Keep notes. You can use the section at the back of this book for doing so. When you return home, sort out your impressions, using your "College Evaluation" checklist in Chapter 7 as a guide. If you don't get a chance to find out all you want to know in the interview, ask your interviewer in a letter. Admissions counselors welcome good questions and are always interested in helping you become better informed.

Chapter 15

Summing Up

When Connie and Jeff met again in the student center snack bar to talk about their day and overnight at Burgess, Connie was glowing, but Jeff was somewhat more subdued.

Although the interview had gone well for Jeff, he had encountered some troubling drawbacks. Along with an anti-fraternity bias, he had found much more academic pressure than he thought he wanted. He had also detected a lack of enthusiasm from history majors about the department's faculty and student interaction, a factor important to him. To top it off, the tennis coach hadn't been encouraging about his making the team. Jeff was going home feeling disappointed and frustrated, with a need to reflect on whether he would even apply to Burgess.

Connie, on the other hand, was excited by what she had found. She didn't much care for a zealous fraternity and sorority system, and Burgess' approach struck just the right note for her. Liberal arts generally, and psychology, English, and science specifically, received excellent reports from students. She especially liked the balance between studies and social activities, and she particularly enjoyed the prospect of being challenged by smart, lively classmates. She had met people engaged in many activities similar to her own interests, and the campus seemed enhanced by the large variety of students coming from all parts of the country. Summing it up, Connie felt good vibes—Burgess had a spirit and ambience that jibed with her desires.

Both Connie and Jeff had done a good job in their investigations. Each had come up with discoveries that filled in the picture of the college, and now each could reach a decision about whether Burgess was a suitable fit.

Getting to the Heart of a College

You won't learn everything about a complex community in a few hours or even overnight, but you can explore all the areas that interest and concern you. Going armed with knowledge about yourself and the college is the basic preparation for the visit, while curiosity and questions are the order of the day when you're on campus.

When you return home, you can sort out your observations and make your analysis of the college's character, its strengths, and its weaknesses. Having gone about the campus visit and interview in an organized, systematic fashion, you will be better qualified to judge whether the college and you make a good match. You will know the real college, and the college will know the real you.

Appendix

College Guides for Specialized Needs

Beckham, Barry, ed. *The Black Student's Guide to College.* New York: E. P. Dutton, 1982.

College and Career Programs for Deaf Students. Washington, D.C.: Gallaudet College, 1986.

Crocker, John R. *The Student Guide to Catholic Colleges and Universities.* New York: Harper & Row, 1983.

Fredman, Ruth Gruber, ed. *Jewish Life on Campus: A Directory of B'nai B'rith Hillel Foundations and Other Jewish Campus Agencies.* Washington, D.C.: The B'nai B'rith Hillel Foundations, 1985.

Howe, Florence, Suzanne Howard, and Mary Jo Boehm Strauss. *Everywoman's Guide to Colleges and Universities: An Educational Project of the Feminist Press.* New York: The Feminist Press at the City University of New York, 1982.

Jarrow, Jane, et al., ed. *How to Choose a College: Guide for the Student with a Disability.* Washington, D.C.: HEATH Resource Center, 1986.

Postsecondary Education and Career Development: A Guide for the Blind, Visually Impaired and Physically Handicapped. Baltimore: National Federation of the Blind, 1981.

Scheiber, Barbara, and Jeanne Talpers. *Campus Access for Learning Disabled Students: A Comprehensive Guide.* Washington, D.C.: Closer Look, 1985.

Other Books from the College Board

College Board. *The College Admissions Organizer.* New York: College Entrance Examination Board, 1986.

College Board. *The College Board Achievement Tests: 14 Tests in 13 Subjects.* New York: College Entrance Examination Board, 1983.

College Board. *The College Cost Book: 1986–87.* 7th ed. New York: College Entrance Examination Board, 1986.

College Board. *Index of Majors: 1986–87.* 9th ed. New York: College Entrance Examination Board, 1986.

College Board. *10 SATs.* 2d ed. New York: College Entrance Examination Board, 1986.

Gelband, Scott, Catherine Kubale, and Eric Schorr. *Your College Application.* New York: College Entrance Examination Board, 1986.

McGinty, Sarah Myers. *Writing Your College Application Essay.* New York: College Entrance Examination Board, 1986.

Mitchell, Joyce Slayton. *College to Career: The Guide to Job Opportunities.* New York: College Entrance Examination Board, 1986.

Notes on Colleges Visited

College _____ Date visited _____

Notes on Colleges Visited

College _____ Date visited _____

Notes on Colleges Visited

College _____ Date visited _____

Notes on Colleges Visited

College _____ Date visited _____